Who Wrote *Shakespeare's* Plays?

Who Wrote Shakespeare's Plays?

WILLIAM D. RUBINSTEIN

AMBERLEY

First published 2012

Amberley Publishing
The Hill, Stroud
Gloucestershire, GL5 4EP

www.amberleybooks.com

British Library Cataloguing in Publication Data.
A catalogue record for this book is available from the British Library.

ISBN 978-1-4456-0190-8

Typesetting and Origination by Amberley Publishing.
Printed in Great Britain.

Contents

1

The Shakespeare Authorship Question

By now, it is well known that many intelligent people – as well as many crackpots – question whether William Shakespeare, the actor and theatre shareholder who was born in Stratford-upon-Avon in 1564 and died there in 1616, wrote the works attributed to him. The aim of this work is to examine objectively the case for believing that someone else wrote Shakespeare's works, as well the case that he did. The author began by believing that, although very difficult to credit, Shakespeare did write the plays attributed to him, but since about 2003 has become fairly convinced that Sir Henry Neville (c.1562–1615), a wealthy MP and courtier who was briefly ambassador to France, actually wrote the works attributed to Shakespeare. The author does not believe that the leading authorised authorship candidates of the present time, Edward de Vere, seventeenth Earl of Oxford (1550–1604) or Sir Francis Bacon (1561–1626), wrote Shakespeare's works. The case that William Shakespeare himself wrote the plays, as the overwhelming majority of scholars believe, is in some respects very strong but in other respects surprisingly weak. All of this will be considered in this work, in as balanced and objective a manner as possible. If this work is seen as anything other than balanced and objective, that is contrary to its purpose.

That William Shakespeare may not have written the works attributed to him is, despite the efforts of all orthodox scholars and biographers to make it seem so, not an absurd proposition, as this work will make clear. Shakespeare was arguably the greatest writer in history, but he is also one, especially considering how intensively his life has been studied, about whom, as an individual human being, remarkably little is actually known. Every orthodox biographer of Shakespeare admits this. 'Of the life of Shakespeare little is known. Most modern lives expand their contents partly by accumulation of details however minute and bearing however remotely on Shakespeare himself; and much more largely by influence and conjecture based on treatment of the plays and sonnets as veiled or unconscious autobiography,' J. W. Mackail wrote in 1934.★ This is emphatically true today, with little to distinguish the biographies of Shakespeare of a century ago from those that roll off the presses several times a year at present. What Mackail said about 'inference and conjecture' from reading Shakespeare's works as autobiographical is also true of many, but perhaps not all, of the works claiming that someone else wrote Shakespeare's works: incidents from the plays or sonnets are seen to be autobiographical accounts drawn from that candidate's life. 'The known facts about Shakespeare's life, as the Heretics [those who believe someone else wrote Shakespeare's works, also termed the anti-Stratfordians] constantly exclaim, can be written down on one side of a sheet of notepaper. Yet his innumerable biographers have managed to spin out versions of his life-story through ponderous works, sometimes in several volumes. One could build up a small library of books about Shakespeare's

---

★ J.W. Mackail, 'The Life of Shakespeare', in Harley Granville-Barker and G.B. Harrison, eds, *A Companion to Shakespeare Studies* (Cambridge, 1934), p.1. Mackail (1859–1945) was Professor of Poetry at Oxford in 1906–11 and the author of *Approach to Shakespeare* (1930).

youth, including for example the 256-page *Shakespeare the Boy* by William J. Rolfe, Litt.D. – a period of his life on which not one single fact is known,' John Michell wrote in 1996.★ Even in the relatively brief period since Michell's work was published, probably fifteen full-scale biographies of Shakespeare have appeared, as well as countless works which rely on a supposed knowledge of the facts of his life, although in the whole of the twentieth century only a handful of new facts have been discovered about Shakespeare, none of which bear on his life as a supposed author.

As well as the paucity of real facts about the most intensively studied of all authors, there is also another main prop supporting those who question whether Shakespeare wrote the works attributed to him: the extraordinary and, to many, impossible gap between the magnitude of Shakespeare's achievement and the meagreness of what is known of his background. In particular, the fact that Shakespeare almost certainly had no formal education after the age of thirteen seems utterly inconsistent with the erudition shown in his works. Shakespeare *appears* to be familiar with many subjects known only to a wealthy, well-educated man of his day, and *appears* familiar with the local geography of Italy, although there is no evidence he ever left England. His two daughters were apparently illiterate. His will famously does not mention his books or manuscripts. The sum total of what survives in Shakespeare's handwriting consists of six signatures on legal documents. If Shakespeare wrote the part of the manuscript of a play entitled *Sir Thomas More* known as 'Hand D', for which there is only questionable evidence, this is the only known literary work in his handwriting. While still in his forties, for unknown reasons, Shakespeare retired from London's cultural

★ John Michell, *Who Wrote Shakespeare?* (London, 1996), p.42.

Renaissance to Stratford-upon-Avon, a provincial town of perhaps 1,300 people, mainly illiterate, to live with his wife, a local girl he married after a 'shotgun' wedding a quarter-century earlier, and his two illiterate daughters, and where he died at only fifty-two, perhaps of boredom. All of this *may* relate to the life of the world's greatest writer, but it is plainly very suspicious. William Shakespeare, the actor and theatre shareholder, seems indeed to have been engaged in the single-minded pursuit of accumulating enough money on the London stage to retire in idleness to Stratford, there to live as (in relative and local terms) a wealthy man, a recognised 'gentleman' with a coat of arms, and the founder of a local landed dynasty – the last aim achieved, because of the death of his son, only in the female line. This is more or less what one might have expected, given Shakespeare's background and roots in Warwickshire, but it seems strangely inconsistent with what one might expect of a writer and intellectual giant of the playwright's calibre.

There is also another factor, often overlooked even by anti-Stratfordians: the sheer implausibility of Shakespeare combining a life as a professional actor and theatre manager with that of being the author of thirty-seven plays (as well as two long poems and over 150 sonnets). The orthodox view of Shakespeare's career was put by Professor James Shapiro in his *1599: A Year in the Life of Shakespeare* (2006).

> Shakespeare and his fellow [theatre] sharers spent their mornings rehearsing and then afternoons performing alongside hired men and boys who were needed to fill out the cast of approximately 15. Except for a break during Lent and the occasional closing of the theatre due to a scandal or plague, performances went on all year round. As Elizabethan audiences expected a different play every day, actors had to master a score of new roles every year – as well as recall old favourites needed to flesh out the repertory.

Especially when plague closed the London theatres, Shakespeare's acting company, the Lord Chamberlain's/King's Men, also went on lengthy tours of provincial towns, and also performed before the Court. On top of all this, Shakespeare maintained two households, in London and in Stratford, and with significant financial interests in both places, which required three days' travelling time to traverse, must have gone from one home to another several times a year. All of these travels and visits were made in England's notorious weather, presumably either on horseback or in primitive carriages, on unmade roads which in recent times would be associated with rural Siberia. Shakespeare's acting performances at the Globe Theatre and elsewhere were also staged out of doors, even in winter, before an audience which must have consisted, at least in part, of drunken louts. Nevertheless, Shapiro espouses the orthodox claim that 'what little free time Shakespeare had at the start of his working day must have been devoted to reading and writing ... [and] providing his company with, on average, two new plays a year'.

This scenario beggars belief. Shakespeare would, unquestionably, have been physically and mentally exhausted by this lifestyle before he wrote a single word. In recent times, it is difficult to point to a single example of anyone who was both a full-time actor *and* a playwright at the same time. It is equally difficult to point to anyone in Shakespeare's time who was also both a full-time actor and a playwright at the same time. Former actors such as Ben Jonson abandoned acting when they became writers. If there were any examples of men from Shakespeare's time who were both, they certainly did not write more than a few plays.★

★ The only contemporary exception to this known to me was Thomas Heywood (1573–1641), who was an actor between about 1598 and 1619, and wrote (it is said) 220 plays alone or in collaboration. Heywood apparently gave up acting in 1619 to concentrate on writing.

Moreover, no one who could earn a reasonable income as a successful playwright would conceivably continue as an actor, with the job's meagre income and utterly exhausting schedule. This would be as if someone appointed from the shop floor to become a director of General Motors voluntarily continued to work night shifts at their auto factory four times a week for the fun of it. It simply wouldn't happen. Once Shakespeare became an established playwright – he apparently earned £6 per play when the annual salary of a schoolmaster was £20, as well as sharing in the profits of the Lord Chamberlain's/King's Men – he would assuredly have abandoned his career as a professional actor. A realistic appreciation of what was actually entailed in the orthodox accounts of Shakespeare's life strongly implies that one is dealing with two separate men, the playwright and the actor.

In addition, there is another reason, also often overlooked, why it is difficult to accept that the Stratford actor wrote the works attributed to him: that, to a remarkable extent, there is no real mesh between his life and the evolutionary trajectory of his works, accepting that the orthodox chronology of Shakespeare's works is valid. What is known about Shakespeare's life has little illuminatory power in explaining why his works evolved as they did. In particular, the real author – whoever he was – appears to have suffered a traumatic experience of some kind about 1601, leading to a comprehensive alteration in the nature of his works: the Italianate comedies and triumphalist histories were replaced by the great tragedies and the 'problem plays'. Many other aspects of the career of the actual author also do not mesh with Shakespeare's life. For instance, he almost certainly could not have read the Strachey Letter, the confidential document about the Bermuda shipwreck of 1610 which was circulated only to directors of the London Virginia Company, and which formed one of the bases of *The Tempest* of *c.*1611. Shakespeare had absolutely no connection with the London Virginia Company, and was not among the 570 men (whose names are known) who purchased a share in the company, let alone a director. As well, he was living in Stratford at the time, not London. Elaborate and preposterous theories have been suggested by orthodox scholars to explain how Shakespeare could have read Strachey's confidential letter, and it is also a mystery as to why he would have written a play, famously his farewell to the theatre, based around the Bermuda shipwreck. Orthodox scholars have long been puzzled by this complete failure of the known facts of Shakespeare's life to mesh in any way with what is in fact the strikingly clear evolutionary trajectory of his works, and, since the 1930s, have given up trying. The complete lack of a nexus between the facts of Shakespeare's life and the pattern of his plays is a major reason why every biography of Shakespeare is unsatisfactory – we are left at the end without an explanation for the genius of Shakespeare's works, while what little is known about the Stratford man appears to point to one whose aims in life are very different, especially given his retirement in comfort as a 'gentleman' in Stratford.

It is also useful to consider just how our knowledge of Shakespeare of Stratford evolved, and how inadequate it really is. While there are many purported contemporary allusions to Shakespeare during his lifetime, they seldom or never convey any information directly linking William Shakespeare the actor and theatre-sharer who was born and died in Stratford-upon-Avon with Shakespeare the writer. Most of those which are frequently cited were written by sources who probably did not know Shakespeare personally. For instance, Francis Meres' celebrated 1598 list of Shakespeare's plays written up to that time, in his *Palladis Tania: Wits Treasury*, is unquestionably very valuable for the chronological information it conveys. But there is no hint in it that Meres knew Shakespeare personally, any more than he was likely to know the literally dozens of other prominent (and also now forgotten) Elizabethan authors he names. Most, if not all, contemporary allusions to Shakespeare are of this sort. To take one example, John Weever's *Ad Gulielmum Shakespeare* (1599), a well-known sonnet beginning 'Honie-tong'd *Shakespeare* when I saw thine issue / I swore *Apollo* got them and none other' is a tribute to the writer known as William Shakespeare but conveys no hint that its author, who had lived in Lancashire and Cambridge (although in the 1600s he did live in London), ever met Shakespeare: it is simply a tribute to his work, just as I might write a glowing poem about a living author I admired without having met him, except through his writings. The *only* apparent reference to Shakespeare during his lifetime as a writer by someone who may have known him is the celebrated reference by Robert Greene in *Greene's Groatsworth of Wit* (1591) to the 'upstart Crow, beautified with our feathers, that with his *Tygers hart wrapt in a Players hyde*, supposes he is as well able to bombast out a blanke verse as the best of you: and being an absolute *Iohannes fac totum* [Jack of all trades] is in his own conceit the only Shake-scene in the countery'. The line cited is from *Henry VI Part III*, but whether the criticism is aimed at a writer or an actor is unclear, just as it is unclear why Greene is warning 'three gentlemen' (usually taken to be university-educated playwrights such as Marlowe), and why they needed to beware of Shakespeare, when dozens of new playwrights appeared every year, is also unclear. In any case, it is certainly not clear that that Greene, even if he wrote the pamphlet (also attributed to Henry Chettle), actually knew Shakespeare. Ben Jonson's criticisms of Shakespeare, in *Conversations with William Drummond*, that 'Shakespeare wanted Arte', were written down in 1618–19, after Shakespeare's death, just as his more famous 'I remember the Players have often mentioned it as an honour to Shakespeare, that in his writing (whatsoever he penn'd) he never blotted out line [*sic*]', and that 'I lov'd the man, and doe honour to his memory (on this side Idolatry) as much as any', appeared in a notebook known as *Timber: or Discoveries; Made Upon Men and Matter* and were apparently not written down until 1626–30 or later, after the appearance of the First Folio, which Jonson probably edited. According to E.K. Chambers, Jonson's 'earlier notebooks perished in a fire of 1623. Probably *Timber*, which contains references to events of 1626 and 1630, is all later' (E.K. Chambers, *William Shakespeare: A Study of Facts and Problems*, Vol. II (Oxford, 1930), p.210). *Timber* was not published until 1641. Of direct anecdotage about Shakespeare in his lifetime, there is almost nothing whatever. In 1599, Sir George Buc (or Buck, *c.*1562–1632), who had the reversion of the post of Master of the Revels, wrote the following of the anonymous play *George a Greene, the Pinner of Wakefield* (a 'pinner' was a dog catcher). The marginal note of a copy of the play states: 'Written by … a minister, who ac[ted] the pinners part in it himself. *Teste* [testified by] W. Shakespea[re]. Ed Iuby saith that the play was made by Ro. Gree[ne].' There are several important points here. First, Buck consulted Shakespeare, who was certainly an experienced actor and a theatre-sharer. His testimony does not mean that he was a writer. We do not know the circumstances under which Shakespeare was consulted, and there is no evidence that he was ever consulted on authorship questions again. Secondly, the next line 'Ed Iuby saith that the play was made by Ro. Gree[ne]' is virtually never quoted in biographies of Shakespeare. Plainly, Buck did not wholly trust Shakespeare, or could not remember what he said about the name of the author. Since Robert Greene had apparently libelled Shakespeare in his *Greene's Groatsworth*, it seems strange that Shakespeare would not remember

Greene's name. Greene, moreover, was certainly not a 'minister'. Thirdly, that this was written down by Buck is not confirmed in Chambers' *Shakespeare* (Ibid., p.201), which attributes the comments to 'anonymous', and states only that it was written 'in two early 17th century *hands*' on a copy of the play.

Another contemporary who apparently came close to citing Shakespeare as a writer was the playwright Thomas Heywood (*c*.1574–1641). In *An Apology for Actors* (1612), he wrote the following concerning the use of two of his 1609 poems in *The Passionate Pilgrim* of 1612. *The Passionate Pilgrim* was a miscellaneous collection of poems, originally published in 1599 as 'By W. Shakespeare'. In 1612 it was reissued with two poems originally printed in Heywood's *Troia Britannica* in 1609, again by 'W. Shakespeare'. In 1612 Heywood wrote, 'Here, likewise, I must necessarily insert a manifest injury done me in that worke, by taking the two Epistles of *Paris* to *Helen*, and *Helen* to *Paris*, and printing them in a lesser volume, under the name of another, which may put the world in opinion I might steale them from him; and hee to doe himselfe right, hath since published them in his own name: but as I must acknowledge my lines not worthy his patronage, under whom he [William Jaggard, the printer] hath publisht them, so the Author I know much offended with M. *Jaggard* that (altogether unknown to him) presumed to make so bold with his name.' As a result, Jaggard removed Shakespeare's name from the unsold copies.

There are many curious features of this passage, apart from its ambiguity, so typical of Elizabethan/Jacobean writing. 'The Author' was 'I know much offended' with Jaggard, but Heywood does not say how he knew, and the phrasing strongly suggests second-hand knowledge. As well, both editions of *The Passionate Pilgrim*, although published as 'By W. Shakespeare', contained material by other writers, including Christopher Marlowe,

Richard Barnfield, and Bartholomew Griffin, about whose inclusion Shakespeare apparently had no qualms, despite the fact that the attribution to him of their authorship was false. Nor did Heywood comment on this anomaly. All of this is very curious; the main point is that Heywood probably had Shakespeare's negative opinion at second hand.

There is also the mysterious Epigram 159 in *The Scourge of Folly*, written around 1610 by John Davies of Hereford (*c*.1565–1618):

> To our English Terence, Mr. Will. Shakespeare
>
> Some say (good *Will*) which I, in sport, do sing,
>
> Hads't thou not plaid some kingly parts in sport.
>
> Thou hadst bin a companion for a *king*;
>
> And, beene a king among the meaner sort.
>
> Some others raile; but, raile as they thinke fit,
>
> Thou hast no rayling, but a raigning Wit:
>
> *And* honesty *thou sow'st, which they do reape:*
>
> *So, to increase their* Stocke *which they do keepe.*

The meaning of this strange poem is, as Chambers (Ibid., p.214) states, 'cryptic'. Of what 'king' was Shakespeare ever a 'companion'? What do the last two lines mean? Despite the facetious tone, it is unclear if Davies ever knew Shakespeare. He is plainly trying to convey something of an unusual nature about Shakespeare, but *what* is not entirely clear. Anti-Stratfordians have pointed out that Terence was a Roman author of comedies which, according to Diana Price, bore his name but were written by two other writers, Scipio and Laelius.

Rather remarkably, *that's it*. There is literally nothing else written in Shakespeare's lifetime which directly links the Stratford man with the plays he allegedly wrote – no contemporary anecdotes, no mention in diaries or letters, no letters, diaries, or manuscripts by Shakespeare.

The conviction that Shakespeare wrote the works attributed to him hinges on a number of factors, chiefly that his name is on the title page of many of the plays that were published separately as quartos in his lifetime, and, above all, the First Folio of 1623, with its famously amateurish portrait, and the introductory material, especially the poems by Ben Jonson, with the references to Shakespeare having 'small Latine and lesse Greeke', and to his being the 'Sweet Swan of Avon!' To many, all this seems absolutely conclusive: there is plainly no 'authorship question' since it cannot be doubted that Jonson and the others involved in producing the First Folio believed that the Stratford actor wrote the plays. To others, a continuing and perhaps growing minority, this was simply part of a deliberate effort to disguise the real writer, which had presumably been decided upon well before the publication of the First Folio. To them, William Shakespeare was the frontman for the real author, the producer/director and facilitator of his plays by the Lord Chamberlain's/King's Men, his acting company.

In fact, virtually everything which can be found about the supposed events of Shakespeare's life were only set down long after his death, and may or may not have any basis in reality. For a surprisingly long time, no one took the slightest interest in Shakespeare's life and no one bothered to speak to his relatives or neighbours in Stratford-upon-Avon, or to consult any documents about his life. Shakespeare, in fact, did not become the English National Poet until the mid-eighteenth century or later, long after anyone who might have known him had died. The first minor attempts to write anything at all of a factual nature about Shakespeare's life were made by Revd John Ward (1629–81), Vicar of Stratford, who in a notebook (written in

1662 or 1663 but not printed until 1830) stated that he 'heard' that 'Mr Shakespeare was a natural wit, without any art at all; he frequented the plays all his younger time, but in his elder days lived at Stratford: and supplied the stage with 2 plays every year, and for it had an allowance so large, that he spent it at the rate of £1,000 a year as I have heard.' This account of Shakespeare's productivity is surprisingly accurate, but his large 'allowance' seems certainly a wild exaggeration. Ward also reported the familiar story that Shakespeare had a 'merry meeting' with Ben Jonson and Michael Drayton, contracted a fever, and died, again a story with no supporting evidence.

Ward was followed by John Aubrey (1626–97), the famous diarist. Aubrey collected information about Shakespeare, writing it down about 1681. Aubrey apparently discussed Shakespeare with William Beetson (d.1682), an actor whose father, Christopher Beetson, had been a member of the Lord Chamberlain's Men, although we do not fully know from where Aubrey derived his information or how accurate it was. According to Aubrey, Shakespeare's father was a butcher, and, despite Ben Jonson, Shakespeare 'understood Latin pretty well: for he had been in his younger years a schoolmaster in the country'. But Shakespeare's father was not a butcher, and there is no evidence of any kind that Shakespeare had ever been a schoolmaster, who normally had to be a graduate of Oxford or Cambridge, and Shakespeare certainly never attended a university. Aubrey also stated that Shakespeare 'did act exceedingly well', although he was certainly not a renowned actor, and 'was wont to go to his native Country [county, i.e. Warwickshire] once a year', and that he left his money to his sister, which is certainly untrue. But Aubrey does state that Shakespeare was from Stratford-upon-Avon, went to London when he was 'I guess about 18' (which contradicts his claim about Shakespeare being a schoolmaster), became an actor and wrote successful plays. Aubrey was writing about sixty-five years after Shakespeare's death, and it was already clear that a completely accurate biography of Shakespeare was by then impossible, and would inevitably mix fact and fantasy.

The first biography of Shakespeare, about 2,000 words long, did not appear until 1709, ninety-three years after his death. This appeared as the Introduction to Nicholas Rowe's (1674–1718) *Works of William Shakespeare*. Rowe (who in 1718 became Poet Laureate) sent Thomas Betterton (*c.*1635–1710), an actor and his son-in-law, to Stratford to secure what information he could about Shakespeare. Rowe's biography, compiled decades after anyone who could possibly have remembered Shakespeare had died, contains much accurate information, such as that Shakespeare's father was John Shakespeare, 'a dealer in wool', and that he had two surviving daughters. But he also states that Shakespeare left Stratford for London because he had 'fallen into ill company' and poached Sir Thomas Lucy's deer; that Queen Elizabeth 'commanded' him to write a play about Falstaff in love, hence *The Merry Wives of Windsor*; and that the Earl of Southampton 'gave him a thousand pounds, to enable him to go through with a purchase which he heard he had a mind to', stories which might charitably be described as apocryphal, and for which no supporting evidence exists.

But solid research was about to become more normal. In 1747, Joseph Greene (1712–90), Master of Stratford Grammar School, became the first man since Shakespeare's time to read his will. Probably no single fact about Shakespeare research better describes the near complete lack of interest in Shakespeare's life for several generations than this fact, that no one anywhere bothered to track down and read Shakespeare's will until 131 years after his death. Greene sent a transcription of the will to James West (*c.*1704–72), Secretary to the Treasury and later President of the Royal Society, but the will did not appear in print until 1763, when it featured in a publication called *Biographica Britannica*. Greene was also the first man to consult the Stratford Registers, and, for the first time, ascertained the date of Shakespeare's baptism. Again, no one had bothered to research this until more than a century and a quarter after Shakespeare's death.

It was about this time, or perhaps slightly later, that the flood of research about Shakespeare began in earnest, such that by the end of the Victorian period Shakespeare had probably become one of the most intensively studied human beings in history. By our time, literally every scrap of paper surviving from Shakespeare's lifetime has been pored over in an effort to find something – anything – about his life, and above all his purported life as a writer. But there is a rule without apparent exception that the more intensively Shakespeare's life is studied, the less is found. Indeed, in the whole of the twentieth century, only two new pieces of information about Shakespeare of any significance have been found by the army of researchers engaged in Shakespearean scholarship. The first was the Belott–Mountjoy Lawsuit, discovered in 1909 in the Public Record Office by Charles William Wallace and his wife Hilda Alfreda Wallace. Charles William Wallace was a professor at the University of Nebraska, and the couple lived in London for much of the time between 1907 and 1916, where they examined *five million* original records in public archives in an attempt to find new Shakespeare evidence. Apart from some interesting original findings about Shakespeare's holdings in the Globe and Blackfriars theatres, their major discovery was the Belott–Mountjoy Lawsuit, at which, on 11 May 1612, Shakespeare gave evidence and signed the deposition. The lawsuit concerned a promised dowry owing to Stephen Belott, apprentice to a Huguenot tire maker (a manufacturer of women's headdresses) in Cripplegate ward, whose daughter he married. William Shakespeare had lodged with Mountjoy around eight or ten years earlier, and was called to give evidence. In essence, Shakespeare stated that he could remember little or nothing about the case, signed the written deposition of the lawsuit, and went about his business. He is described in the deposition as 'William Shakespeare of Stratford upon Avon in the County of Warwick, gentleman'; the deposition says nothing whatever about his supposed career as a playwright or his career as an actor – nothing whatever. Presumably he lodged with Mountjoy when he was actively connected with the Lord Chamberlain's/King's Men. Shakespeare's signature on the deposition was the sixth authentic one known, and the last to be discovered.

From the 1920s, and especially since the 1940s, there has emerged the 'Shakespeare in Lancashire' thesis, that as a youth Shakespeare spent two years in the households of two gentry families in rural Lancashire, those of Alexander Houghton and Sir Thomas Hesketh; Houghton was a Catholic. This thesis arose from the legacy left by Houghton in 1581 to a 'William Shakshafte' (*sic*) who 'now dwelleth with me'. In recent years, thanks in large part to the excellent work by Professor E.A.J. Honigman, *Shakespeare: The 'Lost Years'* (1985), a veritable school of publications has arisen claiming that Shakespeare was a secret Catholic, that he was sent to this remote Catholic household probably through the efforts of a schoolmaster at Stratford who was from Lancashire, and that, from Lancashire, Shakespeare attached himself to Lord Strange's Men (later Lord Derby's Men) and went on to London and immortality. Like Falstaff's 'eleven buckram men grown out of two', but massively larger, all of this emerges from two words in a will, which on the face of it refer to someone else. There is some indirect evidence that Shakespeare and his family may have been secret Catholics, but the evidence on the other side is far greater: Shakespeare was baptised, married, and buried as a conforming Anglican, and is buried in a prominent place in an Anglican church. His two surviving daughters married Anglicans, one a well-known Puritan, Dr John Hall. If Shakespeare was indeed a secret but sincere Catholic, he would presumably have married his daughters to other Catholics via some underground network of recusants or converts. Even apart from this, there is no evidence of any kind that Shakespeare ever spent even one day in Lancashire, unless he went on tour there with his acting company. None of the legends and tales about Shakespeare's early life mentions Lancashire, and most state that life in Stratford became too hot for him, perhaps as a deer poacher, and he hit the high road to the capital, as so many tens of thousands of others have done down the ages.

Again, believe it or not, *that's it*. Apart from these two discoveries – the second of which is very likely a red herring – *nothing whatever* – absolutely nothing – has been discovered about Shakespeare's life in the past century, despite the army of researchers who have attempted to find something – anything – bearing on his life. Apart from these two pieces of evidence, nothing whatever is known about Shakespeare's life which was not known to the Victorians. If there are any exceptions to this conclusion, they are very minor ones, such as documents concerning John Shakespeare's Stratford business or the like. Emphatically, absolutely nothing has been discovered in the past century or more bearing in any way on Shakespeare's supposed career as a writer.

As Diana Price has cogently noted in her *Shakespeare's Unorthodox Biography: New Evidence of an Authorship Problem* (2001), this lack of real evidence about Shakespeare's career as a writer contrasts strikingly with the evidence which exists about many if not most of his contemporary writers of note. In virtually every case, as Price makes clear, actual evidence survives which makes it absolutely clear that they were writers and known personally by others to have been writers. For instance, shortly after Christopher Marlowe's death, Thomas Kyd stated that he was 'writing for his [Lordship's] Players'. Ben Jonson left behind handwritten manuscripts. He was imprisoned for writing *The Isle of Dogs* and *Eastward Ho!* Jonson was termed 'my beloved friend that singular Poet Mr Ben Jonson' by John Selden in 1614. He was, of course, buried in Westminster Abbey as 'O rare Ben Jonson'. Thomas Nashe left behind a handwritten verse in Latin and in a letter referred to his 'writing for the stage and for the press'. Michael Drayton was termed 'excellent poet' in the notebooks of Dr John Hall, who treated him. Hall was Shakespeare's son-in-law but apparently made no mention of Shakespeare's literary activities. Thomas Dekker, Thomas Heywood, Nathan Field and others were paid by name by Philip Henslowe for writing plays, whereas nothing like this survives for Shakespeare. And so on, and so on. Shakespeare, according to Price, has *less* in the way of an existing 'paper trail' about him than perhaps any notable writer of his time. But even Diana Price appears to have missed the point that this discrepancy exists despite the fact, noted above, that Shakespeare has been more intensively studied by researchers, by a factor of many orders of magnitude, than any of his contemporaries. If an equivalent 'paper trail' exists for Shakespeare even remotely similar to that of his fellow authors, it should clearly have been discovered long ago and become common knowledge. But none has ever been discovered and apparently does not exist.

In addition to these points, there are a number of other important considerations about the life of Shakespeare which ought to be considered by anyone interested in the authorship question, and which deserve to be examined in detail.

The Chronology of Shakespeare's Works

A vital consideration in understanding the authorship question is the chronology of Shakespeare's works: when, and in what order, he wrote his plays and poems. There is universal agreement among orthodox scholars that the order in which he wrote his works was not random, but shows a clear pattern of development and evolution. The first attempt to produce a chronological listing of Shakespeare's works was made in 1778 by Edmund Malone (1741–1812), the greatest Shakespeare scholar of the eighteenth century, whose 'Attempt to Ascertain the Order, in which the Plays of Shakespeare were written' was published as part of a complete edition of Shakespeare's plays edited by George Steevens, another eminent eighteenth-century scholar. Malone's list is regarded as largely but not wholly accurate, for instance dating *Hamlet* to 1596 rather than 1601 and *King Henry VIII* to 1601 rather than to 1613. But it does begin with the three *Henry VI* plays in 1589–91 and dates *The Tempest* to 1612 (followed by *Twelfth Night*, dated to 1614, rather than its now accepted date of 1599–1601).

Over the next 150 years, a commonly accepted chronology of Shakespeare's works became fixed, especially through Sir E.K. Chambers' seminal two-volume *William Shakespeare* (1930). The accepted order of the writing of Shakespeare's works is as follows:

1589–90	*1 Henry VI*
1590–91	*2 Henry VI*
	3 Henry VI
1592–93	*Richard III*
	Titus Andronicus
1593–94	*The Comedy of Errors*
	The Taming of the Shrew

1594–95	*Two Gentlemen of Verona*
	Love's Labour's Lost
1595–56	*Romeo and Juliet*
	Richard II
	A Midsummer Night's Dream
1596–97	*King John*
	The Merchant of Venice
1597–98	*1 Henry IV*
	2 Henry IV
1598–99	*Much Ado About Nothing*
	King Henry V
	The Merry Wives of Windsor
1599–1600	*As You Like It*
	Twelfth Night
1600–01	*Hamlet*
1601–03	*All's Well That Ends Well*
	Othello
1603–04	*Measure for Measure*
1604–05	*Timon of Athens*
1605–06	*King Lear*
	Macbeth
1606–07	*Anthony and Cleopatra*
1606–07	*Coriolanus*
1608–09	*Pericles*
1609–10	*Cymbeline*
1610–11	*A Winter's Tale*
1611–12	*The Tempest*
1612–13	*King Henry VIII*
1613–14	*Two Noble Kinsmen*

There were, in addition, Shakespeare's poems, *Venus and Adonis* (1593), *Rape of Lucrece* (1594), the *Sonnets* (published in 1609), and his minor poems.

The most recent modifications in the accepted chronology were made by Stanley Wells and Gary Taylor in their *William Shakespeare: A Textual Companion* (1987), who generally accept the previous dating but, for instance, believe that Shakespeare's earliest plays were *The Two Gentlemen of Verona* (1590–91) and *The Taming of the Shrew* (1590–91), and who also attempt to date two probable lost plays of Shakespeare's, *Love's Labour's Won* (1595–96) and *Cardenio* (1612–13), the latter co-authored with John Fletcher and derived from Cervantes' *Don Quixote*.

The accepted dating of Shakespeare's works is based on a wide variety of considerations. For instance, contemporary sources and references to the plays, such as Francis Meres' celebrated listing of twelve of Shakespeare's plays known to him in 1598, are crucial pieces of evidence. So, too, are changes in Shakespeare's stylistics, such as the ratio of rhyme to verse and the use of 'colloquialisms' (such as 't, i'th, o'th, th', and 'em), which evolve in a consistent and traceable manner throughout Shakespeare's career. No orthodox scholar, and certainly very few others, radically dissent from this general chronology.

There are several striking conclusions to be derived from the commonly accepted chronology of Shakespeare's works. First, as Edward Dowden (1843–1913), an eminent professor of English Literature, was the first to observe (in 1875), Shakespeare's works evolve according to a fairly consistent pattern. In the first half of his career – to the writing of *Hamlet* around 1601 – Shakespeare wrote his Italianate comedies and triumphalist English histories. For whatever reason, there was a radical and discernible break in the direction of Shakespeare's works around 1601, when, within a few years, he wrote *Hamlet* and the other great tragedies.

From about 1604, he wrote the so-called 'problem plays' such as *Measure for Measure*, and a 'romance' (as such plays are known), *Cymbeline*, before reaching a closure of some kind in *The Tempest*, apparently his last sole-authored play. Accounting for this clear and consistent pattern of development, and why Shakespeare's works evolved as they did, has simply stumped his biographers. There was, for instance, simply no known traumatic event in Shakespeare's life to explain why he should have written *Hamlet* and the other great tragedies in about 1601 to 1606, and this is – as will be suggested below – one of the keys to coming to terms with the authorship question. The accepted chronology of Shakespeare's works also shows his growth and deepening as a playwright, with, for instance, the villainous character of Richard III marking a new level of development on his previous main characters, with more subtle and memorable figures such as Shylock, Portia, Hamlet, and Lady Macbeth following as his career evolved. As well, it seems that although Shakespeare was a tireless writer, producing around thirty-seven plays in less than twenty-five years, many of which are among the greatest works in literature, in the second half of his career he generally produced only one play per year, rather than two per year (as was the case earlier in his career). Shakespeare also appears to have retired from playwriting a few years before his death in 1616, possibly for reasons of ill health, although we simply do not know why.

This well-established chronology of Shakespeare's works has very important implications for the authorship question, that is, to those who claim that someone else, such as the Earl of Oxford or Sir Francis Bacon, wrote Shakespeare's works. If their preferred authorship candidate did not live at almost precisely the same time as William Shakespeare, whose words, according to all authorities, were written between *c.*1590 and *c.*1613, they must devise an entirely new chronology for explaining when that candidate supposedly wrote Shakespeare's works. This is particularly the case with the Earl of Oxford, who was born in 1550 – and was thus around forty when Shakespeare's first work appeared, according to the normal chronology – and died in 1604, nine years before Shakespeare's last play was written. Not only must they devise an entirely new chronology, for which the evidence is dubious or non-existent, but they must also invent a plausible evolutionary trajectory for their candidate's writings as 'Shakespeare', not merely some scattergun pattern whereby an early Shakespeare play was followed by a late one, or vice-versa. The chronological element is very important to the plausibility of the case that Shakespeare wrote the works attributed to him; if he did not, the actual author must have had virtually identical dates, or an enormous amount of (non-existent) evidence must be found to support an entirely different chronology.

That the accepted chronology is accurate is supported by other real evidence. For instance, all of the quarto editions of Shakespeare's plays (stand-alone printed versions) appeared between 1594 and 1609, much as one might suppose if the standard chronology is accurate, but quite different from the dating one might expect, for instance, if the seventeenth Earl of Oxford was the actual author.

Shakespeare's Education and Learning

There appears to be a gross incongruity between, on the one hand, Shakespeare's educational background and what his contemporaries thought of his erudition, and, on the other hand, what one can reasonably infer about this from his writings. Shakespeare in all probability attended Stratford Grammar

School, probably to the age of thirteen, where he was taught to read Latin. There was one appointed schoolmaster for the whole school in addition to one or two junior schoolmasters for the younger students. The names of the successive schoolmasters of his time there are known; all were university graduates, as were most if not all schoolmasters, even in little-known provincial schools. Shakespeare also learned rhetoric, but was taught nothing about English literature or anything else. He had no known schooling past the age of thirteen. Indeed, according to Shakespeare's first biographer Nicholas Rowe (1674–1718) in 1709, Shakespeare was taken out of Stratford Grammar School when the fortunes of his father, John Shakespeare, a local glove maker and wool dealer, declined. Shakespeare certainly did not attend a university (of which only two, Oxford and Cambridge, existed in England), as he does not appear in comprehensive lists of matriculants at the two universities.

Those of Shakespeare's contemporaries who commented upon his education and learning were not impressed by it. Ben Jonson, an erudite classical scholar, famously said that he had 'small Latin and less Greek'. Francis Beaumont claimed that Shakespeare wrote 'by the dimme light of Nature'. Thomas Fuller (1608–61), whose *Worthies of England* was published in 1662, a work which may have been based on interviews with persons who knew Shakespeare, claimed that Shakespeare 'was an eminent instance of the truth of that Rule, *Poets non fit, sed nascitur*, one is not made but *born* a poet. Indeed, his learning was very little, so *nature* itself was all the *art* which was used upon him.' In contrast, there is no surviving contemporary or near-contemporary statement which claims that Shakespeare was a well-educated man. The only possible exception to this was John Aubrey (1626–97), who, in his *Brief Life* entry on Shakespeare, noted that 'though as Ben Jonson says of him, that he had little Latin and less Greek, he understood Latin pretty well, for he had been in his younger years a schoolmaster in the country' (modernised spelling). Although Aubrey claims this, no one has ever found a record of Shakespeare having been a 'schoolmaster in the country', a position generally restricted to university graduates.

The problem with all of this is that it is evident from everything in Shakespeare's works that their author was an incredibly learned and erudite man. The claim that Shakespeare wrote 'by the dimme light of Nature' suggests something like a pre-literate Welsh or Icelandic bard who created a national saga from his imagination despite being illiterate and without books or sources. But it is obvious from everything in the Shakespearean canon that its author was extraordinarily well read, and used hundreds of both well-known and obscure sources in his works. A recent compilation of *Shakespeare's Books: A Dictionary of Shakespeare's Sources*, by Stuart Gillespie (2001), examines over 200 ancient and modern sources used by Shakespeare, several of which had not yet been translated into English when Shakespeare used them. Virtually all of Shakespeare's works, in fact, are based to a greater or lesser extent on previous published sources which have been traced by recent scholars. Shakespeare used some sources more than others: most of his English history plays (and others) derive from *The Chronicles of England, Scotland, and Ireland* by Raphael Holinshed (*c.*1529–*c.*1580) and from *The Union of the Two Noble and Illustre [sic] Families of Lancastre and Yorke* by Edward Halle (*c.*1498–1547), but Shakespeare effortlessly used literally dozens of sources in writing his works. Shakespeare's commanding erudition has been obvious to critics for centuries past and at the present time. For instance – to take one example – in the most recent (2006) Arden edition of *As You Like It*, its editor, Juliet Dusinberre, notes, 'It would not be difficult to gain the impression from reading any commentary on *As You Like It* that this is a play which demonstrates that its author was dauntingly well read, and that the drama itself demands a well-read audience … But though the play can be enjoyed in the study, it never creates the impression – unlike some of Ben Jonson's plays – that it was conceived there.' Where did Shakespeare read the many sources upon which his works were based? No one knows. There were no public libraries, Shakespeare's will does not mention any books he owned, and no book ever owned by Shakespeare has ever been found, either owned by members of his family or by someone else. Critics have suggested that Richard Field (d.1624) – the London printer who was born in Stratford, probably knew Shakespeare, and printed three of his poems – owned a library which Shakespeare used, but there is not a shred of evidence either that he did or that Shakespeare's sources were books owned by Field. Others have suggested that Shakespeare used the library of a nobleman in London such as Lord Burghley or Lord Southampton, but, again, there is simply no evidence that he did, or that an unknown provincial actor would have been allowed to use a nobleman's private library.

There is, in other words, a major incongruity between Shakespeare's apparent lack of erudition – a point made and affirmed by contemporaries who knew him – and the fact that his plays show extraordinary learning and erudition, totally inconsistent with an author who wrote 'by the dimme light of Nature'. We seem to be dealing with two entirely different men: the poorly educated but naturally witty and clever actor/theatre sharer of London, and the deeply learned man who wrote his alleged works.

Along with Shakespeare's truly remarkable but effortless erudition is his even more incredible inventiveness of words and phrases, many of which would be widely assumed to be proverbial except for the fact that they were first devised by

Shakespeare. The many common phrases which first occur in Shakespeare's works include 'It's Greek to me', 'more sinned against than sinning', 'to act more in sorrow than in anger', 'vanished into thin air', 'green-eyed jealousy', 'tongue-tied', 'a tower of strength', 'make a virtue of necessity', 'slept not one wink', 'stood on ceremony', 'danced attendance upon', 'laugh yourself into stitches', 'had short shrift', 'cold comfort', 'too much of a good thing', 'seen better days', 'lived in a fool's paradise', 'clear out bag and baggage', 'high time', 'foul play', 'without rhyme or reason', 'bid good riddance', 'dead as a doornail', 'a laughing stock', 'bloody-minded', 'for goodness sake', and 'what the dickens', among hundreds of others. Shakespeare coined hundreds of new words, of which accommodation, assassination, dislocate, premeditated, submerged, and alligator are typical examples. No single person had a more profound impact on the English language. Indeed, it has seemed to some as if Shakespeare – whoever he was – was somehow deliberately trying to replace the classical tongues with English as the universal language of the world, an effort which, thanks to the British Empire and the American republic which emerged two centuries after Shakespeare's time, has been successful. Today, English is, for all practical purposes, the universal language of the world, and Shakespeare has single-handedly replaced the ancient classics as the central touchstone of literature, at least in the English-speaking countries. Indeed, and even more uncannily, it can be argued that by the time of the death of Milton in 1674 English had already produced the most distinguished literature of any culture in the world, with Shakespeare at its centre. Yet Shakespeare emerged from a provincial town of 1,300 people, where the main aim of its local leaders and its local schooling was certainly to produce conformity, enabling Stratford to avoid any trouble with the English government at a time of rapid political, religious, and economic change, with its real hazards and dangers. Shakespeare's background in Stratford-upon-Avon, and his grammar school education there, appear singularly unlikely to have produced his extraordinary linguistic creativity, to say nothing of the most notable feature of his writings, what Keats termed his 'negative capability', that is, his unique ability to empathise with all of his characters, regardless of their marginality or unorthodox viewpoints. Again, there appears to be something very wrong with all of this, a gross incongruity between the man William Shakespeare who was born and died in Stratford-upon-Avon, and the author of his works. These incongruities have not been satisfactorily explained by orthodox scholars, who gloss over them or ignore them altogether.

There are other similar incongruities about Shakespeare's life for which there is no satisfactory explanation. Many scholars, especially native Italians, believe that Shakespeare must have visited Italy, since his knowledge of the local geography of Italian cities, canals, and roads could only have been acquired by an eyewitness. There is, however, no evidence that Shakespeare ever left England or travelled to Italy; certainly his acting companies never did so. Where he acquired his extensive knowledge of Italian geography is a complete mystery. If someone else wrote the plays, however, and if that man is known to have visited Italy, there is no mystery. Orthodox scholars of Shakespeare's life argue that he just might have visited Italy, although there is no evidence that he did, or that he acquired his knowledge about Italy from talking to English travellers in taverns, or perhaps from Italians in London. They do not explain why he bothered to put this detailed knowledge into his plays, for audiences which consisted for the most part of persons who had never visited Italy, and did not care whether his display of erudition about Italian geography was accurate or not.

Shakespeare, London, and Stratford

Although Shakespeare's professional life as an actor, theatre-sharer, and supposed playwright was always centred in London, his aim in life, in so far as we understand it, was always centred in Stratford-upon-Avon, and always revolved around using the money he made in London to become recognised as a gentleman and a 'man of property' in his home town. Shakespeare's father obtained a coat of arms in 1596, probably at the instancing of his son, marking out the family as 'esquires' (those with official coats of arms) and hence of gentle birth. William Shakespeare made extensive purchases of land, property, and tithes (ownership of which yielded an income) in and near Stratford, among them his purchase, in May 1597, of New Place, the second-largest house in Stratford, an impressive residence of 60 feet by 70 feet with ten rooms and extensive gardens. (It was thoughtlessly demolished in 1759 by its owner at the time, Revd Francis Gastrell, who apparently objected to the large number of visitors wishing to see, even then, the home of the Bard.)

In contrast, in London Shakespeare apparently only rented rooms, as he did from the Belotts, Huguenot tire makers (makers of women's headdresses) of Cripplegate ward. The only exception to this came at nearly the end of his life, and apparently long after he ceased to be an actor when, in March 1613, he purchased the Blackfriars Gatehouse for £140. It was close to the Blackfriars Theatre, the indoor theatre used by the King's Men after about 1608–09. Shakespeare then mortgaged the residence to one Henry Walker, its previous owner, for £60. Everything about this purchase is rather mysterious. Shakespeare had three co-trustees, William Johnson, John Jackson, and John Heminges, the last apparently the actor in the King's Men to whom Shakespeare left a legacy in his will. The three co-trustees did not, it seems, put up any money themselves, and the result of this procedure was to deprive his wife Anne of a legal dower or life interest in the property. The Blackfriars Gatehouse had also long been associated with secret Roman Catholic intrigue, a matter of significance to those historians who believe that Shakespeare was a secret Catholic. But it seems more likely that the Gatehouse was purchased as an investment and also, perhaps, as a place of residence for members of the King's Men near their indoor theatre and also not far from the Globe Theatre across the Thames. Shakespeare held no other known investments in London.

Shakespeare's financial life thus consisted of the continuing transfer of his considerable and perhaps growing income from the London theatre (and perhaps from other sources) to Stratford-upon-Avon, where, it seems, he intended to settle during all of his career. He appears to have had remarkably little ego-involvement in the London intellectual world, despite supposedly being at the centre of one of the greatest intellectual renaissances in history. One of John Aubrey's anecdotes about him, apparently written down about 1661, was that 'he was not a company keeper … wouldn't be debauched & if invited to writ, he was in paine'. Although Shakespeare, according to Thomas Fuller, in a work published in 1662, was supposed to have had 'many … *wit-combates* betwixt him and Ben Jonson', and although Shakespeare was supposed to have been a member of the Mermaid Club with other intellectuals (for which there is no real evidence), he appears to have had few real friends among the London intelligentsia. (Fuller claims that while Jonson was 'solid but slow', Shakespeare was distinguished by 'the quickness of his wit', something which he could not possibly have known first-hand, since he was born in 1608 and thus Shakespeare died when he was only seven or eight.) Shakespeare left small legacies in his will to three of his fellow actors, and many large and small legacies to his Stratford relatives, neighbours, and friends, but nothing – not a farthing – to anyone from the London intelligentsia, even Ben Jonson, who subsequently almost certainly edited the First Folio, or John Fletcher, with whom he collaborated on several late plays. He left no one among the London intelligentsia any monetary legacy, and nor did he leave them any books, or the care of any of his manuscripts or papers. It was as if they never existed.

For those who believe that William Shakespeare was an actor and theatre-sharer, but not the author of the works attributed to him, this is not surprising: they did not exist for him, not as intellectual equals and literary comrades. If Shakespeare was simply a very successful actor and theatre-sharer, who apparently had the magic touch in terms of making at least reasonable amounts of money, but wrote no works of literature and had no apparent deep interest in any intellectual activity beyond acting, the thrust of his life's financial transactions becomes much clearer. Shakespeare apparently retired to Stratford by, say, 1612 (and perhaps earlier), when he was only forty-eight, and he lived there with his wife, a local girl he had married twenty-five years earlier after a shotgun wedding, and his two daughters, who were apparently illiterate, in what was a provincial town of around 1,300 persons with few educated men and few intellectual activities of any kind. For the greatest and most creative writer in history, this course of action is almost incomprehensible. For an upwardly mobile former actor and businessman in London, it is not.

Consideration of this also raises the question of how Shakespeare made his money. He had certainly become very rich by the standards of Stratford-upon-Avon. Most of his wealth and income can probably be accounted for by his earnings as a theatre-sharer and actor in London, and he may also have inherited money from his father or from the Arden or Hathaway families. If he was also a playwright and poet, he presumably made some money from his writings, although apparently only £6 per play. (It is unclear whether he or another author made any money from the sale of his works, in Shakespeare's case his poems and quartos of his plays – probably not.) But if Shakespeare also acted as the frontman for the real author, serving as his producer-director in the theatre, and being paid for the use of his name and for keeping silent, this may help to explain where at least a part of his wealth and income came from. If so, this strongly implies, of course, that the real author was at least reasonably wealthy, and was willing to pay for what was apparently his hobby or secret second career. Perhaps the real author earned some of his money back from the theatre takings, although there is no direct evidence for any of this. Certainly, however, Shakespeare's total and central financial focus on returning as a wealthy man to Stratford is abundantly clear.

Shakespeare's Religion

A considerable number of experts about Shakespeare believe that he was a secret Roman Catholic, maintaining the old faith in a Protestant England where Catholics were often tortured and killed. The proponents of this theory have probably increased in number in recent years. There are a number of pieces of evidence that Shakespeare might have been a secret Catholic. At some time between 1688 and his death in 1708, Revd Richard Davies – who lived at Stratford-on-Thames, not Stratford-upon-Avon – wrote down some notes on Shakespeare's life, including the first story that he poached deer from Sir Thomas Lucy, and concluded his notes with the simple remark, 'He dyed a papist.' Davies's evidence or source for this was not given, and nor has it turned up since. In 1784 John Jordan (1746–1809), who was born near Stratford and was another collector of Shakespeariana, claimed in the *Gentleman's Magazine* to have discovered the 'spiritual Last Will and Testament' of John Shakespeare, the father of the Bard, in which he declared himself to be 'an unworthy member of the holy Catholic religion'. Jordan claimed that this six-page testament had actually been found in 1757 by a local bricklayer who was retiling the rafters of a house in Stratford owned by a descendant of Shakespeare's sister. Commentators have since debated the authenticity of this document, whose supposed survival for over 150 years in the rafters of a house belonging to a distant relative of Shakespeare is obviously highly implausible. Recent commentators have, however, discovered that the wording of the document is identical to that of the so-called Borrowes Formulary, a standard Catholic document of the time. John Shakespeare's actual testament, which it is claimed he 'signed' with a glover's mark, has disappeared, so its authenticity cannot be tested with modern scientific methods. There is, thirdly, the 'Shakespeare in Catholic Lancashire' thesis, discussed above. Finally, towards the end of his life Shakespeare purchased the Blackfriars Gatehouse in London, regarded as a haunt of Catholics.

Against this, however, must be set the certain facts that William Shakespeare was baptised, married, and buried as a practising Anglican, and is buried in a prominent position in the local Anglican church. There is little or nothing in Shakespeare's works which would indicate that he was sympathetic to Catholicism, while his history plays champion Tudor triumphalism, with that dynasty's promulgation of the Reformation. Yet in recent years many works advancing the notion that Shakespeare was a secret

Catholic have been produced by both academic and independent scholars. The religious question is therefore of considerable importance to orthodox Stratfordian scholars, especially if Shakespeare was a secret Catholic whose true religious views are embedded ambiguously in his works, as some have suggested. Of course, if someone else wrote the plays, Shakespeare's religion is irrelevant, except perhaps in linking him with the real author or his circle of associates.

What seems clearly to emerge from all this is that there does appear to be a legitimate 'Shakespeare authorship question': at least it does not seem absurd, or evidence of mental illness, to assert that there appear to be many significant anomalies in our knowledge of the life, and particularly the supposed writing career, of William Shakespeare. There simply appears to be dramatically less real evidence about Shakespeare's life, and especially his life as an author, than there 'ought' to be, given what is routinely known of his contemporaries and, especially, the vast amount of research which has been conducted over several centuries by dedicated scholars and researchers with the sole aim of discovering something new about Shakespeare's life, and there are many apparent anomalies about his life. This does not necessarily mean that William Shakespeare did not write the works attributed to him, and there is obviously a great deal about his life – his dates; his undoubted career as an actor and part-owner of the Lord Chamberlain's/King's Men; above all the First Folio and its dedicatory material – which compels recognition of a straightforward acceptance of the orthodox view. But there is also a great deal on the other side, especially the sheer lack of real evidence about his supposed life as a writer. Since at least the mid-nineteenth century, many others have been proposed as the real author of Shakespeare's works. While there is a plausible case to be made in favour of some or most of these as the real author, the case for *and against* each ought to be considered objectively, as will be done below. The same should also be done in the case for and against William Shakespeare as the author of the works attributed to him.

Doubts About Shakespeare –
Initial Doubts and the Baconians

While it is true to say that there was no explicit questioning of the authorship of Shakespeare's works until the nineteenth century, to a surprising extent there were hints about this from a surprisingly early date. This should also be placed in a wider context: no one took a keen or obsessive interest in Shakespeare's life – or any interest at all – until much later, and Shakespeare was not regarded as the supreme English writer until the mid-eighteenth century. Yet there were apparent doubts. The cryptic poem on Shakespeare by John Davies of Hereford and, perhaps most blatantly, the striking apparent reference to 'Shakespeare' as a pseudonym by Thomas Vicars (Sir Henry Neville's son-in-law; see p. 147) in the 1620s, among others, are evidence that some people seem to have had doubts about Shakespeare's authorship in his lifetime or soon after.

The question of who was actually the first person explicitly to deny that Shakespeare wrote the works attributed to him, and when these doubts were first voiced, is a matter of some controversy. It has long been thought that the first man to deny explicitly that Shakespeare wrote Shakespeare was Revd James Wilmot (1726–1808), an Oxford-educated rector, from 1781, at Barton-on-the-Heath, Warwickshire, about six miles from Stratford. Wilmot, according to a later account, tried to find anything in local archives and the private libraries of the local gentry relating to Shakespeare. He allegedly looked in every old private library within a fifty-mile radius. He could find nothing whatever relating to Shakespeare. From this and other aspects of his failure to find anything relating to Shakespeare, Wilmot concluded that Sir Francis Bacon wrote the works. He did not publish his thoughts, but, in 1805, related them to an Ipswich Quaker, James Corton Cowell, who was also collecting local sources relating to Shakespeare, to be read at two meetings of the Ipswich Philosophical Society in February 1805 and April 1806. Cowell's two papers remained a secret for more than a century, until Professor Allardyce Nicoll published extracts from them in the *Times Literary Supplement* in 1932.

While Wilmot and Cowell have thus long been credited with being the first explicit anti-Stratfordians, very recently much doubt has been thrown on the whole episode through the research of Dr John Rollett of Ipswich and of Professor Dan Wright of Concordia University in Oregon, both prominent anti-Stratfordians. It seems that there was no 'Ipswich Philosophical Society', while no one has succeeded in tracing anyone named James Corton Cowell. Yet there was certainly a Revd James Wilmot of Warwickshire, and Cowell's two talks do exist, in handwritten manuscript form, in the Durning-Lawrence collection at London University (the collection compiled by Sir Edwin Durning-Lawrence, an MP and prominent Baconian). If Cowell's two manuscript essays are a hoax, they are certainly a curious and seemingly pointless one.

From the mid-nineteenth century, however, there came a flood of doubters about Shakespeare as a writer: such men as Joseph C. Hart, a New York lawyer, in 1848; Robert Jamieson, writing in *Chambers' Edinburgh Journal* in 1852; and William Henry Smith in 1856. The best-known of these early anti-Stratfordians was Delia Bacon (1811–59), an American who moved to England in 1853 and began a great crusade to convince all and sundry that Shakespeare's works were written by Sir Francis Bacon (no relation). In 1857 she published a 675-page work, *The Philosophy of the Plays of Shakespere [sic] Unfolded.* It was one of the most important anti-Stratfordian works in history, and unleashed a torrent of late nineteenth-century anti-Stratfordians, such as Ignatius Donnelly (1835–1901), a major American politician who was also known as 'the king of crackpots'. It was Donnelly who apparently initiated the search for a secret code in Shakespeare's works which revealed the real author to be Francis Bacon (or someone else). By 1900, the question of who wrote Shakespeare was widely discussed in intellectual magazines such as the *Fortnightly Review*, and anti-Stratfordianism attracted the support of many gifted men, including Mark Twain and Sigmund Freud.

The Earl of Oxford and Others

It would not be long until other authorship candidates entered the scene. The most important of these was Edward de Vere, seventeenth Earl of Oxford (1550–1604), the most popular alternative candidate today, who was first proposed by the unfortunately named J. Thomas Looney (pronounced 'Loney') in 1920 in his *'Shakespeare' Identified.* Looney, a schoolmaster in Gateshead, tried to infer the characteristics of the 'real' author of Shakespeare's works from characteristics about the writer which could be drawn from his plays. (See the section below on the Earl of Oxford for a fuller discussion.) Looney became convinced that the English aristocrat Edward de Vere wrote the plays, and that the main characteristics of his life supported this view. Looney argued for Oxford's 'candidacy' notwithstanding the fact that he died nine years before Shakespeare's last play was written, according to the normal chronology of Shakespeare's works, and that there is nothing – literally nothing – to connect Oxford with Shakespeare, his acting company, or Shakespeare's associates, while all the evidence – for instance his opposition to the Essex rebellion in 1601 – suggests that he had no connection with Shakespeare and his circle.

The 'Oxford' movement grew among a coterie in England and America, but probably took on renewed life and vigour only comparatively recently. Many of today's Oxfordians credit their reading of Charlton Ogburn Jr's *The Mysterious William Shakespeare* (1984) with setting off their interest in the authorship question and in Oxford, as well as the *Frontline* television debate on the authorship question, 'The Shakespeare Mystery', aired on American public television in 1989. Other works and events also kept this subject alive, such as the much publicised efforts by Calvin Hoffman, author of the pro-Marlowe work *The Murder of the Man who Was 'Shakespeare'* (1955), to find Shakespeare's manuscripts in the tomb of Sir Thomas Walsingham in 1956 (although he secured permission to open the tomb, he found only sand).

By the 1960s, the entire question, with its ambience of pseudo-scholarship somewhat suggestive of late Victorian séances, threatened to disappear. But, as noted, it has returned with a vengeance, and there are probably now more active anti-Stratfordians than ever before. As arch-Stratfordian James Shapiro claims in his *Contested Will* (2010), the internet, and the possibilities it raises for instantaneous worldwide networking and publicity, are probably a major reason for the recent escalation in interest, but certainly not the whole reason. Anti-Stratfordianism has its roots, as was made clear above, in the extraordinary gap between the meagreness of Shakespeare's background and the magnitude of his work, as well as in the sheer inability of generations of researchers to discover anything about his supposed career as a writer, and the many other anomalies about his life. Orthodox Stratfordians are fond of saying that anti-Stratfordianism is based on 'snobbery', an inability to credit a grammar school boy from the provinces, rather than a nobleman, with the ability to produce Shakespeare's works, but this is an egregious red herring which ignores the central fact that Shakespeare's life remains a near-complete blank, while the learning evident in his works strongly implies a well-educated man (not necessarily a nobleman) as the real author.

The Academics and the Amateurs

The snobbery, indeed, is all on the side of the Stratfordians. This was not by any means always true, but is a relatively recent development closely related to a fundamental change which has occurred in the study of Shakespeare by scholars and researchers. Until well into the twentieth century, most Shakespearean scholars were well-educated amateur scholars who were employed in another profession and studied Shakespeare and his works as a passionate hobby. For instance, Edward Malone (1741–1812), Shakespeare's first biographer, was a barrister; James Halliwell-Phillips (1820–89), one of the leading nineteenth-century Shakespeare scholars, was librarian of Jesus College, Cambridge; Howard Staunton (1810–74), author of *Memorials of Shakespeare* and the first to publish a photographic reprint of the First Folio, was a journalist and the unofficial World Chess Champion; and so on. Even in the first part of the twentieth century, Sir E.K. Chambers (Edmund Ketchever Chambers, 1866–1954), probably the greatest of all Shakespeare scholars, was a senior civil servant in the Department of Education who, until his retirement, undertook his monumental research in his spare time. This lack of *academic* interest in Shakespeare very arguably had the effect of making for freer discussion, with fewer taboos. While today Stratfordian academics dismiss anti-Stratfordian theorists as 'mere amateurs', until the First World War or later virtually *all* Shakespeare scholars were 'mere amateurs', yet nearly everything we know about Shakespeare's life emerged from their 'amateur' research, while none of today's taboos on the authorship question existed. These issues were freely debated in intellectual journals of the period.

Possibly the first eminent writer on Shakespeare who was employed as a university academic in the modern sense was Ernest Dowden (1843–1913), who was Professor of English at Trinity College, Dublin from 1867 to 1913. The career of Sir Sidney Lee (1859–1926) marked a transition: from 1883 to 1913 he was assistant editor and then the second editor of the *Dictionary of National Biography* and wrote its entry on William Shakespeare. From 1913 to 1924 he was Professor of English at London University, at which point the academics crowd out the amateurs. Since the Second World War, and emphatically since the 1960s, the great majority of scholarly writers on Shakespeare have been university academics. There have been some exceptions whose work is recognised by academic scholars, such as Eric Sams and Ian Wilson, but these have become vanishingly rare. While in many respects this change represents a gain for our understanding of Shakespeare, it has meant that 'amateur' speculation on the authorship question is treated with contempt. Amateur speculation threatens the established place of academics as the custodians of true knowledge, and also threatens to introduce 'crackpot' speculation (which, of course, is an apt description of many anti-Stratfordians) into the accepted order of academic things. As many academic Shakespeare scholars freely admit, an anti-Stratfordian article has as much chance of being read at an academic conference on Shakespeare, or of being published in an academic journal on Shakespeare, as a 'Creationist' interpretation of the natural world has of being published in an academic journal on biology. The only long-term antidote to this state of affairs lies in significant numbers of academics seriously raising the Shakespeare authorship question in an informed way. This appears to be in the process of occurring, with university academics in America, Britain, and in Europe now prepared to engage with the real possibility that someone else wrote the works attributed to Shakespeare. This is not to say that they are necessarily right, only that the issue deserves to be debated rationally, not automatically denied a hearing *per se* as taboo, which has been the situation up to now.

Certainly the informed public is now readier to debate this question than at any time in previous decades, as evidenced by the popularity of anti-Stratfordian conferences, societies, and published works. Increasing numbers of orthodox academic scholars, including Stanley Wells and James Shapiro, have launched recent counter-attacks on anti-Stratfordianism, rather than treat its proponents with silence and contempt. What is undeniably missing, however, is any real and direct evidence that someone else wrote Shakespeare's works, although the entire issue emerged because there is also so little convincing evidence that Shakespeare wrote the works attributed to him.

This book will now consider the claims *for and against* the leading alternative candidates as the real author of Shakespeare, as well as the claims of William Shakespeare himself. So far as the author is aware, this has never been attempted before, and the aim throughout has been to be objective, although dubious and spurious claims and arguments will always be exposed as such.

2

William Shakespeare

What little is known about the life of William Shakespeare is universally known. He was born in Stratford-upon-Avon in 1564, the son of John Shakespeare (d.1601), a glove maker who also dealt in wool and other commodities, and who served as bailiff (mayor) of Stratford in 1571, and as chief alderman and a justice of the peace. Wiliam's mother, Mary Arden (d.1608), was the daughter of a farmer and small landowner in Wilmcote, about three miles away, and was distantly related to the Ardens of Park Hall, an ancient gentry family. William Shakespeare had four sisters and three brothers, one of whom, Edmund (1580–1607), also became an actor in London. Shakespeare was presumably educated, probably to the age of thirteen or so, at Stratford Grammar School; he had no further education, so far as anyone knows, and did not attend a university. In 1582 he married Anne Hathaway (c.1556–1623), from a minor landed family, after a 'shotgun' wedding, producing a daughter, Susanna (1583–1649), and then twins Hamnet (1585–96) and Judith (1585–1662) – Hamnet was named for a Stratford friend, Hamnet Sadler – but no other children.

The next period in Shakespeare's life is a complete blank, the only exception being a mention in a Bill of Complaint in 1588, in which William Shakespeare and Shakespeare's father and mother offered to buy some property from a relative, Edmund Lambert. (This Bill of Complaint is seldom mentioned in biographies of Shakespeare, possibly because it might suggest that he was in Stratford at the time.) What he was doing during the 'lost years' has given rise to endless speculation, ranging from his working as a tutor in Catholic gentry families in Lancashire, to training as a lawyer or being employed as a 'schoolmaster in the country'. The best known account is that, possibly because of some misdeed such as poaching deer, he came to London, held horses at the theatre door, and then joined a theatre company as an actor and then a playwright.

It appears that Shakespeare began writing plays around 1588–89, and was, apparently, attacked by name in 1592 in Robert Greene's posthumous *Greene's Groatsworth of Wit*. Shakespeare achieved some popularity with his two long poems, *Venus and Adonis* (1593) and *Rape of Lucrece* (1594), both dedicated to the Earl of Southampton, and wrote many plays for the Lord Chamberlain's Men, with which he was connected as an actor and a theatre-sharer. In 1596 he was granted a coat of arms. In 1598 Francis Meres named twelve of Shakespeare's plays in his *Palladis Tamia*. Shakespeare gradually built up a considerable property holding in Stratford and lived there in a large house, New Place. In 1609 his *Sonnets* were published by Thomas Thorpe. His last plays were written in 1612 and 1613; in the latter year he was the purchaser, or one of the purchasers, of the Blackfriars Gatehouse in London. In April 1616, at the age of only fifty-two, he died, of unknown causes; his will makes no mention of any books or manuscripts. He was buried, with a striking monument, in Stratford church. In 1623 thirty-six of his plays, including eighteen previously unpublished plays, were printed in a large volume universally known as the First Folio.

Apart from this, virtually nothing more is known of Shakespeare's life, aside from what, with any other noted writer, would be regarded as wholly insignificant. For instance (as noted above), in 1612 he gave evidence in what is known as the Belott–Mountjoy lawsuit, a lawsuit brought for failure to provide a promised dowry from the family of a couple, the Mountjoys, with whom he had been lodging in 1604; Shakespeare gave brief evidence and signed the deposition, in which he was described as 'of Stratford upon Avon … gentleman', rather than as a writer or an actor. Beyond this, virtually nothing more of a definitive nature is known of Shakespeare's life, and virtually nothing which throws any light upon his alleged career as a writer – virtually nothing whatever.

Points in Favour of William Shakespeare as the True Author

1. His name is on the title page – Shakespeare's name is on the title page of most (not all – some are anonymous) of his writings published in his lifetime and in the First Folio of 1623, along with his portrait and poems and other material praising him. This is, manifestly, *prima facie* evidence that he wrote the works attributed to him, just as it is with any author. Of course, some authors write under pseudonyms, but the use of the name of one living man – there is not the slightest doubt that William Shakespeare existed – to camouflage another man being the real author is probably without parallel. Such a case would be categorically different from the ordinary uses of a pseudonym, for instance 'Mark Twain' for Samuel Langhorne Clemens. There was no actual man known as 'Mark Twain'; he did not exist, except in the

mind of Samuel Clemens. For an actual living man, William Shakespeare, to have been the frontman for another man, the real author, would, as noted, be probably unique in literary history.

2. A frontman could not exist long in the real world – Any frontman who was *also* an actor and a full participant in a major acting company would have found it almost impossible, and perhaps absolutely impossible, to make anyone believe that he was the actual author of plays they performed if he wasn't. He would have been constantly asked about the plays he allegedly wrote. It would be blatantly obvious within weeks (or days) to other members of the acting company that this William Shakespeare was not the actual author of the plays. The actor William Shakespeare would, moreover, presumably have met at frequent intervals with the real author. The real author would have had to be fully informed about the available members of the theatre company, as well as whether a play he intended to write was acceptable to the company. The real author would presumably expect to be paid; even if he were very rich, he would nevertheless have to come to some working arrangement about finance with the theatre company. There is the further question of just what the role of the actor William Shakespeare was in all this – did he act as the real author's producer, director, or what? – and what the real author's relationship was with the rest of the company, especially with its senior members. The entire enterprise would surely have foundered as a secret in a very short time.

3. In Shakespeare's lifetime or soon afterwards, he was credited with being an author – Although the number of contemporaries who clearly stated that Shakespeare wrote the plays attributed to him are certainly less than one would ideally

like to have, they do exist, from the 'Shake-scene' reference in *Greene's Groatsworth of Wit* to Ben Jonson's tributes, and his statement, made in his *Discoveries* around 1630, that 'the Players often mentioned it as an honour to *Shakespeare*, that in his writing (whatsoever he penn'd) he never blotted out line [*sic*]'. Francis Meres thought in 1598 that Shakespeare was a major playwright, and so did the other contributors of verses to the memory of William Shakespeare in the First Folio: Hugh Holland, Leonard Digges, and 'I.M.' So, too, did Shakespeare's acting colleagues John Heminges and Henry Condell, who wrote an introduction to the First Folio. Many of these opinions were written after Shakespeare's death, but by men who in most cases certainly knew him well.

4. The evidence of the First Folio – The celebrated First Folio of 1623 is an elaborate tribute to William Shakespeare (described as the 'Sweet Swan of Avon'), and illustrated with a famous, if rather inadequate, portrait by Martin Droeshout. What conceivable object would there be in creating this sincere (and expensive) tribute to Shakespeare if he was not a great author but only a minor, provincial actor? Why would anyone, seven years after his death, claim that he wrote the plays if he didn't?

5. His dates are right – William Shakespeare was born in 1564 and died in 1616. All recognised scholars believe that his works were written between 1588–90 when Shakespeare was in his mid-twenties, and 1613, three years before he died. This is exactly what one would expect if he was the author of the works attributed to him.

6. No one questioned that he was the author – There were no 'anti-Stratfordians' until the nineteenth century (although, as noted above, this point is contested by anti-Stratfordians). Given Shakespeare's prominence even during his lifetime,

if he were not the real author this would have been well known almost at once. That it allegedly remained a secret for over two hundred years seems incredible.

7. There are autobiographical hints in Shakespeare's works – These have been seized upon by Stratfordians, and include the alleged use of Warwickshire dialect; the use of the name 'Hamlet' (very similar to the name of Shakespeare's son, and also the name of Katherine Hamlett of Tiddington near Stratford, who drowned in the Avon in 1580, obviously similar to the death of Ophelia); the apparent reference in *The Merry Wives of Windsor* to the coat of arms of Sir Thomas Lucy, whose deer Shakespeare allegedly poached; his knowledge of the work of glove makers, his father's occupation, and of the routine in local grammar schools; and other indications of this kind. In *The Taming of the Shrew* Christopher Sly says 'Ask Marian Hacket, the fat ale-wife of Wincot, if she knew me not.' This Wincot is probably a village four miles from Stratford, where, in November 1591, the parish register records the baptism of 'Sara Hacket, the daughter of Robert Hacket'. No other alleged author but William Shakespeare is likely to have heard of Wincot. These pieces of evidence are not blatant or conclusive, but occur often enough as to indicate when Shakespeare was writing from personal experience.

8. Shakespeare is unique in having his own identity as a writer questioned – No one claims that Dante, Goethe, or Tolstoy were frontmen for someone else, nor Milton, Wordsworth, Dickens, or T.S. Eliot. Anyone who asserted that they were would be asked to produce conclusive evidence for the claim or be branded a lunatic. With Shakespeare, and Shakespeare alone, it has for at least 150 years been open season for crackpots who deny his obvious identity, yet can produce

no compelling evidence whatever for their claims. Moreover, they often rely on alleged secret codes in the writings, and weird theories, such as the 'Prince Tudor' theory of some Oxfordians (see below), to support their claims.

9. Whoever wrote the plays had to be a man of the theatre – Shakespeare's plays are pre-eminently theatre pieces, written with an expert knowledge of the realities of the theatres used by the Lord Chamberlain's/King's Men and of the members of these companies and of their strengths. Only an insider member of the Lord Chamberlain's/King's Men could have had this detailed, hands-on knowledge. The plays were written quite explicitly for Shakespeare's company and its actors. An amateur outsider, a dilettante nobleman or the like, would simply not have had this detailed knowledge.

10. The Stratford monument – The famous Stratford monument to Shakespeare, inside Stratford parish church and adjacent to his tomb, was erected by 1623, when it is definitely mentioned in a poem in the First Folio by Leonard Digges, whose stepfather, Thomas Russell, was one of the overseers of Shakespeare's will, and lived four miles from Stratford. It is thus very likely that Digges would have seen Shakespeare's monument at some time before 1623. The well-known early drawing of the tomb by William Dugdale in 1653 admittedly looks little like its current appearance, but the inscription below Shakespeare's bust is likely to be identical to what it is today, since it begins with the same words. (In Dugdale's drawing, only the first two words of the Latin inscription appear.) The inscription translated and modernised reads: 'In judgement a Nestor, in genius a Socrates, in act a Virgil … with in this monument [is] Shakespeare; with whom quick nature died … all that he hath writ, leaves living art but page to serve his wit.' (The first part of the inscription is in

Latin, the latter part in English; of course Shakespeare is not buried within the monument but adjacent to it.) Nothing could be clearer than this, a clear tribute to Shakespeare as a great writer. This monument must have been in place by 1653, when Dugdale drew it, and presumably by 1623, when Digges mentioned it in his poem.

11. Richard Field – Richard Field was the London printer who produced Shakespeare's first published works, *Venus and Adonis* in 1593, *The Rape of Lucrece* in 1601, and *Phoenix and Turtle* in 1601 (as part of Robert Chesterton's *Loves Martyr*). Field (1561–1624) was from Stratford-upon-Avon, the son of a tanner with whom Shakespeare's father did business. It seems obviously likely that they knew each other, and it would certainly be a remarkable coincidence if Shakespeare were not the real writer, but Field, from the same small town, published his early poems.

12. '2 plays every year' – One point in favour of Shakespeare is seldom made by his supporters. Revd John Ward, the Vicar of Stratford 1662–81, wrote in his notebooks, kept in 1662–63, a number of remarks about Shakespeare, including the 'merry meeting' story. One paragraph (with its spelling modernised) reads as follows: 'I have heard that Mr. Shakespeare was a natural wit, without any art at all; he frequented the plays all his younger time, but in his elder days lived at Stratford, and supplied the stage with 2 plays every year, and for it had an allowance so large, that he spent at the rate of £1000 a year, as I have heard.' Prior to 1601, Shakespeare did write two plays a year, although after 1601 his rate of publication was around one play a year. What is important in Ward's remarks is that no one attempted to draw up a chronology or timetable for Shakespeare's plays until Edward Malone did in 1778, more than a century later – when the notion that

Shakespeare did produce two plays a year in the early part of his career first gained currency. Ward's chronology, compiled in Stratford-upon-Avon, does seem very accurate, at least for part of Shakespeare's career. On the other hand, part of his paragraph seems much more dubious. Shakespeare probably did not live full-time in Stratford until his very last years, and it is difficult to see who provided his 'allowance' of £1,000 (or more) a year, an impossibly vast sum. Nevertheless, the point about '2 plays every year' seems highly pertinent.

13. 'Shake-scene' – The first apparent reference to Shakespeare as a playwright occurred in *Greene's Groatsworth of Wit Bought with a Million of Repentence,* allegedly the deathbed remarks of Robert Greene (1558–92), an Oxford-educated playwright. In it he said 'Yes, trust them not: for there is an upstart Crow, beautified with our feathers, that with his *Tygers hart wrapt in a Players hyde,* supposes he is as well able to bombast out a blanke verse as the best of you: and being an absolute *Iohannes fac totum* [Jack of all trades] is in his own conceit the only Shake-scene in the countrey'. This passage was apparently addressed to other university-educated playwrights, warning them against Shakespeare. The words about the 'Tygers hart …' is a parody of a line in *Henry VI Part III*, usually said to have been written in 1590–91. Orthodox historians claim that this is an obvious reference to Shakespeare as a playwright. The passage is so ambiguous, however, that others are not so sure: why would Greene warn three university-educated playwrights against Shakespeare when many non-university-educated playwrights (Ben Jonson, for example) came to prominence every year? Does the passage even refer to Shakespeare, and is it not a criticism of him as an actor, not a playwright? And why would Robert Greene – if he was indeed the author of the passage, which is now

widely attributed to Henry Chettle (*c.*1560–1607) – have regarded Shakespeare so bitterly? Nevertheless, this has long been viewed as direct evidence that William Shakespeare was indeed a playwright.

Points Against William Shakespeare as the True Author

1. Shakespeare had no real qualifications to write the works attributed to him – His works contain literally hundreds of references to classical and recent writings, some of which (such as Belleforest's *Histoires Tragiques* and Cinthio's *Epita* and *Hecatommithi*) had not been translated into English. According to Italian scholars who knew Italy well, his plays set in Italy contain many details of local geography which could only have been known to an eyewitness visitor to Italy, but there is no record, of course, of his having ever left England. Shakespeare knew of Galileo's astronomical discoveries before they were generally known in England. He had access to the Strachey Letter, about the Bermuda shipwreck of 1609, although it was a confidential document available only to directors of the London Virginia Company. He apparently had accurate knowledge of a range of subjects, including the law (his knowledge of the law has long been praised by lawyers), medicine, seamanship, and other specialised subjects. It is obviously very difficult to see how he could have acquired this knowledge, since he had no formal education past the age of thirteen. It is also very difficult to see why he should have packed such erudition into his plays. It is difficult as well to see where Shakespeare obtained the more obscure books he used, since there were

no public libraries at the time, or how and why he would obtain books in foreign languages he couldn't read.

2. Shakespeare could not have been both an actor and a writer – This is a point which is frequently overlooked by both sides in this debate. Shakespeare apparently remained a professional actor until perhaps 1604, after he had written many of his plays. He was thus a full-time actor and playwright for possibly fifteen years. As an actor he would have acted in different plays several times a week, gone on frequent tours to the provinces, and acted before the Court. At the Globe (or any other outdoor theatre) he would often have been half-frozen and played in front of audiences of drunken louts. By 1604 he had also allegedly written up to twenty-four plays. As noted, this beggars belief: a professional actor would have been physically and mentally exhausted before he put pen to paper. Significantly, there were virtually no major Elizabethan or Jacobean dramatists who were *also* actors; if there were any, they (like Ben Jonson) quickly abandoned acting for writing, or wrote only a few plays while they remained as actors. Only Shakespeare is alleged to have done both.

3. The lack of mesh between Shakespeare's life and the trajectory of his plays – This is a most important point, also often overlooked by both sides in the debate. By the orthodox chronology of the plays, Shakespeare's evolutionary trajectory was unusually clear: prior to 1601 he wrote the Italianate comedies and the triumphalist histories; from about 1601 he wrote the great tragedies and the 'problem plays', before reaching closure in *The Tempest*. Unfortunately, little or nothing can be inferred from Shakespeare's actual life to account for this. In particular, there is nothing in Shakespeare's life to account for the great break around 1601. Orthodox

scholars have attempted to account for this by reference to the death of Shakespeare's son Hamnet in 1596, but this occurred five years earlier and in the interim Shakespeare wrote the Falstaff plays, or by reference to the death of Shakespeare's elderly father in 1601, although Shakespeare was thirty-seven at the time and not close to his father. Most scholars believe that Sonnet 107, which begins 'The mortal moon hath her eclipse endur'd', refers to the death of Queen Elizabeth in 1603, and that Shakespeare was glad when she died, but why should he have been? During her reign he had risen from unknown provincial to a well-known and prosperous playwright and theatre-sharer. Orthodox biographers are at a loss to explain how Shakespeare obtained the Strachey Letter of July 1610, used as one of the bases of *The Tempest*, given that the document was only circulated privately to directors of the London Virginia Company, a body with which Shakespeare had absolutely no connection. There are many other similar incongruities between Shakespeare and his supposed works. In other words, one cannot infer very much, if anything, about Shakespeare's writings from the known facts of his life. The plain implication is that one is dealing with two different men, the author and the actor.

4. Shakespeare's lack of interest in literary matters – As is well known, the only examples of Shakespeare's handwriting are six signatures on legal documents, although some scholars believe (without convincing evidence) that 'Hand D' (as it is known) in the manuscript of a play, *Sir Thomas More*, probably written in either 1592–93 or 1603, is in Shakespeare's handwriting. No other literary works, letters, signatures, or documents of any kind by Shakespeare have ever been discovered; nor has any book definitely known to have been owned by him. Again as is well known, his

will makes no mention of any literary works or books. In his will, Shakespeare did leave 26 shillings 8 pence each to John Heminges, Richard Burbage, and Henry Condell, three of his fellow actors in the Lord Chamberlain's/King's Men, specifically to buy rings which clearly demonstrates that he was certainly closely connected with this acting company, but left nothing to any author, even Ben Jonson and Michael Drayton, who supposedly had a 'merry meeting' with Shakespeare just before his death. He left nothing to John Fletcher, with whom he had allegedly recently collaborated, nor to his townsman Richard Field, who printed three of his poems. He had nothing whatever to say about his manuscripts or books, if these existed. This complete lack of interest in literature by the man who is universally regarded as the world's greatest writer is certainly puzzling. It is, however, fully consistent with the William Shakespeare who died in Stratford in 1616 being an actor, but not a writer.

5. Remarkably little is known of Shakespeare's life, and especially of his supposed life as a writer. William Shakespeare was not merely a writer; he is one of the most intensively researched and studied human beings in history. Every scrap of paper from his lifetime has been scoured to try to find something which bears on Shakespeare's life, and especially his alleged life as a writer, but nothing ever turns up. During the entire period since 1900, essentially only one or two new pieces of information have emerged about Shakespeare's life, most notably the Belott–Mountjoy lawsuit of 1612, discovered in 1910, and the will of Alexander Houghton, a Catholic landowner in Lancashire, indicating that Shakespeare might have spent two years as a boy actor or page in a Catholic household in Lancashire. Even that is debatable, since Houghton's will refers to a 'William Shakeshafte', not

'Shakespeare'. Apart from these two discoveries, *absolutely nothing* has been discovered since 1900 about Shakespeare's life, and especially about his alleged life as a writer. Given the number of qualified and keen researchers who have, since 1900, researched Shakespeare's life and the literary life of Elizabethan England, this is surely remarkable. The clear inference from this is that nothing has been discovered because there is nothing to discover.

6. The contrast in information between Shakespeare and other writers of his time – This lack of information about Shakespeare's life as a writer should be contrasted with the significant knowledge we have in most other cases of well-known writers living at the same time as Shakespeare. For instance, a royal pension awarded to Ben Jonson was increased in 1630 in consideration of 'Those services of his wit and his pen'. The Merchant Taylors Company in London states that it was 'to confer with Mr. Benjamin Johnson [*sic*] the Poet, about a speech'. In 1597 Jonson was imprisoned for writing *The Isle of Dogs*. Many other references from his lifetime exist acknowledging that the man Ben Jonson was a poet and playwright, just as they exist for most of Shakespeare's other contemporary writers. It is precisely this contemporary identification of William Shakespeare of Stratford as a writer which does not exist, and certainly not in the clear and unambiguous fashion one might suppose. This appears to be the case even in the introductory material to the First Folio, probably edited by Ben Jonson. Apart from Jonson's famous 'Sweet Swan of Avon' poem, verses praising Shakespeare appear by three men: Henry Holland, Leonard Digges, and 'I.M.', who is generally thought to be James Mabbe. There is no evidence that Holland or Mabbe ever met Shakespeare, although Digges's mother had remarried Thomas Russell, an

overseer of Shakespeare's will. None of the three poems praise Shakespeare as a human being or comment on any aspect of his personal merits. None of the three was a major poet or writer. Strikingly, Jonson did not solicit or procure verses from writers of note who may actually have known Shakespeare, such as Michael Drayton, John Fletcher (who collaborated with Shakespeare on some of his last plays), or John Donne, a member of the Mitre Club, to which Shakespeare may have belonged. Nor did he obtain commendatory verses from the Earl of Southampton, Shakespeare's old patron; from William Herbert, third Earl of Pembroke, the Lord Chamberlain and co-dedicatee of the First Folio; or from Richard Field (d.1624), Shakespeare's fellow Stratfordian, who published three of Shakespeare's poems. Indeed, it appears as if Jonson went out of his way to obtain verses in Shakespeare's honour specifically from rather obscure men who did not know him, or knew him only vaguely, and who never praised him as a human being. Although seldom remarked upon, this action is deeply suspicious.

7. Much of what is supposedly known about Shakespeare is apocryphal – Despite the fact that less is known about Shakespeare's actual supposed life as a writer than about most of his contemporaries, what pass for facts about his life, and are regularly repeated in biographies of Shakespeare, are often very dubious. To take some examples, the claim that Shakespeare, Michael Drayton, and Ben Jonson had a 'merry meeting' where the playwright 'drank too hard' and 'died of a fever there contracted' comes from the notebook of Revd John Ward (1629–81), who was Vicar of Stratford from 1662 to 1681, and was written in his notebook sometime between February 1662 and April 1663 – forty-six or forty-seven years after Shakespeare's death (and thirty-one years after the

death of Drayton and twenty-four years after the death of Jonson). There is no prior mention of this anecdote in any source and Ward noted in the previous paragraph that he should 'Remember to peruse Shakespeare's plays ... That I may not be ignorant in this matter.' Ward's anecdote *may* be true, although it is unsupported by any credible evidence. The first biography of Shakespeare did not appear until 1709, nearly a century after his death, when Nicholas Rowe published a brief life of the playwright. This biography is the first to claim that Shakespeare had to flee from Stratford because he was 'engaged ... more than once in robbing a park that belonged to Sir Thomas Lucy' (not, as is often is recounted, poaching his deer), that he played the ghost in 'his own *Hamlet*', and that Lord Southampton 'gave him a thousand pounds to enable him to go through with a purchase', a familiar anecdote which is almost certainly false, as Southampton was nearly impoverished at the time. Rowe's source for the Southampton anecdote 'was handed down by Sir William D'Avenant', who apparently claimed to be Shakespeare's illegitimate son and died in 1668, more than forty years before Rowe's work was published. In other words, these familiar stories about Shakespeare's life are highly dubious and lacking in any credible confirmatory evidence. Yet they are endlessly repeated in most biographies of the playwright.

8. The meagreness of direct evidence for Shakespeare as the author in his lifetime – The actual evidence by his contemporaries that William Shakespeare, the Stratford actor, actually wrote the works attributed to him is surprisingly meagre. In his widely reviewed *Contested Will* (2010), James Shapiro offers a chapter on why Shakespeare actually wrote the plays. Apart from indirect evidence – for instance, many

editions of his plays were published in his lifetime, with his name on the title page, and his authorship was never challenged – Shapiro produces some actual evidence to prove his point. George Buc (or Buck), Master of the Revels from 1610 to 1622, inquired about the authorship of a play published in 1599, *George a Greene, the Pinner of Wakefield* (a 'pinner' is a man who catches stray animals, a dog catcher). On the title page of the quarto edition of the play, Buc wrote, 'Written by ... a minister, who ac[ted] the pinners part in it himself. *Teste* [attested by] W. Shakespea[re]'. Presumably Buc met Shakespeare and asked him about the play. As Shakespeare was a major theatre-sharer and an actor in London, and had been for many years, there is nothing remarkable in this. What it does not show – as Shapiro implies it does – is that Shakespeare wrote *Hamlet* or anything else. Shakespeare, as an actor, knew that the author was a 'minister' and had acted in his own play (which, incidentally, is surely unusual if not impossible), but not, it seems, the name of the playwright. Nor did Buc ever ask Shakespeare anything else about London playwrights; he is not mentioned in anything else Buc wrote which survives. Buc also notes that 'Mr. Shakespeare' and 'Richard Burbage' were each paid 44 shillings by the Steward to the Earl of Rutland for designing an *impresa* used by the earl in 1613 to celebrate the accession of James I. An *impresa* was a heraldic design displayed in banners and paper shields. This reference may not have been to William Shakespeare at all, but to the King's 'bit-maker', one John Shakespeare, but even if William Shakespeare is meant, this obviously has no bearing whatever on whether he wrote *Macbeth*. Shakespeare's ability as a designing artist is otherwise unknown, of course, and remarked upon by no one. Most alleged contemporary references to Shakespeare

are of this type – very dubious – and apparently clutching at straws in the absence of better evidence.

Similarly dubious are the claims that 'Warwickshire dialect' is used in Shakespeare's plays, evidence that the author came from there. No one today knows the extent, or even the nature, of 'Warwickshire dialect' in the late sixteenth century; this 'dialect' may well have existed in other parts of England and later vanished, especially that which was spoken in rural areas near London, swallowed up by the growth of the capital. The first real 'dialect' dictionaries date from Victorian times, and cannot give an authoritative picture of linguistic differences three hundred years earlier.

9. The lack of interest in Shakespeare's life until long after his death – Shakespeare did not become the English National Poet until the late eighteenth century, and, to a remarkable extent, no one took any real interest in his biography until long after his death. Perhaps the most extraordinary example of this is that no one bothered to read his will until 1747, when Joseph Greene (1712–90), Master of Stratford Grammar School, discovered a copy of Shakespeare's will in Stratford (where, precisely, is unknown) and sent a transcription to James West, Secretary to the Treasury and later President of the Royal Society. Even then, no one bothered to publish Shakespeare's will anywhere until 1763, when it appeared in the sixth volume of *Biographica Britannica*. Greene was also the first to copy out Shakespeare's baptismal entry from the Stratford Registry. In other words, what we would now regard as the most basic of all accurate information about Shakespeare's life was unknown for over 130 years after his death. This was surely ample time for any false conclusions about the authorship question to have long taken root. As is well known (and has been noted above), Shakespeare's will

contains no information or statement of any kind bearing on his supposed life as a writer.

10. The Stratford bust – For those who think there is no 'authorship problem', perhaps the most (as it were) concrete way of showing that there is something wrong somewhere is by reference to Shakespeare's bust in Stratford church, which was apparently erected soon after his death in 1616. In 1653, William Dugdale (1605–86), an antiquarian who at the Restoration became Norroy King-at-Arms and was knighted, visited many old churches and other sites in Warwickshire, and in 1656 produced his *Antiquities of Warwickshire*. This includes a drawing of Shakespeare's monument in Stratford church, which was later reproduced without change or comment in editions of Shakespeare's works down to the mid-eighteenth century. The problem here is that the Dugdale picture looks absolutely nothing like the bust which is there today. It plainly depicts someone who did not bear the slightest resemblance to the William Shakespeare portrayed in the bust today, a man who has his hands on a sack, possibly a sack of wool. More importantly, the man depicted is not holding a pen, as the man in the bust today is doing, nor a piece of paper on which he is presumably writing a play. The man in the Dugdale picture is much thinner, and looks every inch the suspicious village tradesman rather than the great writer. The illustration of Dugdale's bust in Nicholas Rowe's 1709 edition of Shakespeare also depicts a man with his hands on a sack, but with no pen or paper. By 1737, however, a sketch by George Verture clearly shows a man with a pen.

Some anti-Stratfordians have concluded that the man with the sack drawn by Dugdale was John Shakespeare, William's father, who was a Stratford wool dealer, and that, needless to say, the bust we see today was added later, and in order to give credence to the legend of the Stratford man as playwright. Orthodox biographers of Shakespeare generally have little to say about this egregious discrepancy – it is not discussed in either Samuel Schoenbaum's *Shakespeare's Lives* (1991) or in James Shapiro's *Contested Will* (2010) – but those who do comment on it simply assert that many of Dugdale's drawings were inaccurate, and that this illustration was probably drawn in a dim light. But Dugdale knew that the bust depicted the (by then) famous playwright, and was hardly likely to miss an obvious quill pen and paper, or to depict the great writer with his hands on an apparent sack of wool. Even to sceptics of sceptics, there certainly appears to be more to this than meets the eye.

11. The 'night of errors' and others – Shakespeare's *The Comedy of Errors* was produced at Gray's Inn on 28 September 1594. This was probably its premiere. After the play was performed, the audience, presumably consisting mainly of young lawyers and law students, degenerated into a melee which became known as the 'night of errors'. It is likely that Francis Bacon wrote the accompanying masques, and Shakespeare, whoever he was, the play. But there is a major anomaly about this performance. According to the Chamber Accounts, which give details of payments for entertainment performed at Court, on that very night the Lord Chamberlain's Men, of whom William Shakespeare the actor was certainly a member, were not at Gray's Inn, but six miles downriver, performing at Greenwich Palace before the Queen. The entry in the Chamber Accounts mentions Shakespeare by name as acting at Greenwich. It is *possible* that the Chamberlain's Men rushed, exhausted, from Greenwich to Gray's Inn; it is also possible – as the few pro-Stratfordians who have discussed this anomaly suggest – that there is some confusion as to the

dates, although the entry in the Chamber Accounts seems perfectly clear. Moreover, *The Comedy of Errors* contains sixteen main parts, and the Chamberlain's Men probably consisted of no more than twelve actors, making it most unlikely that it split in two. It does thus seem very likely that William Shakespeare was six miles away when one of his own plays was being premiered, although he was certainly a professional actor at the time whose play would surely have been performed by his own company. The evident inference here is that someone besides William Shakespeare wrote *The Comedy of Errors*.

There are many other incongruities and anomalies of the same kind in Shakespeare's life. For instance, *Shakespeares Sonnets* was registered with the Stationers' Company on 20 May 1609. Several of its sonnets specifically forgive a friend who had done their author great harm, and, previously, Shakespeare had written the famous lines about 'the quality of mercy is not strained'. On 7 June 1609, however, William Shakespeare was in Stratford-upon-Avon, where he successfully sued a man named John Addenbrooke for the recovery of a debt of £6, with 24 shillings of interest. Addenbrooke apparently held the licence to sell starch in Warwickshire. The spiteful pettiness of Shakespeare's lawsuit seems to contrast most incongruously with the humane charity of the *Sonnets* published only a few weeks earlier. Can this really be the same man? (On the Addenbrooke lawsuit, see Katherine Duncan-Jones, ed., *Shakespeare's Sonnets* (1997), p.12; E.K. Chambers, *William Shakespeare: A Study of Facts and Problems*, Vol. II (1930), pp.114–18; and Samuel Schoenbaum, *William Shakespeare: A Documentary Life* (1975), pp.183 and 192.)

12. The 'dimme light of Nature' – Ben Jonson famously claimed that Shakespeare had 'small Latin and less Greek', and Francis

Beaumont wrote in 1615 that he wrote 'by the dimme light of Nature'. They both apparently believed that Shakespeare was poorly educated, and that his lack of education was a notable feature of his persona. Yet most orthodox biographers of Shakespeare argue the very opposite, that Shakespeare's education in the classics at Stratford Grammar School was a superior one, and is fully able to account for the extraordinary erudition shown in Shakespeare's works. They cannot both be right, and it is the great learning shown almost casually in Shakespeare's works which surely requires an explanation, as well as why Jonson and Beaumont thought the opposite. (See the section on Sir Henry Neville for an alternate explanation.)

13. The Junius test – A number of anti-Stratfordians have suggested an interesting test of whether Shakespeare wrote the plays. Suppose the author of Shakespeare's plays was genuinely unknown, like the real author of the eighteenth-century *Letters of Junius*, and, like Junius, was the subject of endless debate and dispute among scholars. If this were the case, could anyone in his senses believe that William Shakespeare, the Stratford-born actor, was their actual author? A man who had no formal education after the age of thirteen, emerged from a humble background in a small provincial town, was by profession an actor rather an author, whose two daughters were illiterate, made no mention of manuscripts or books in his will, and of whom no known handwriting survives except for six signatures on legal documents? The self-evident answer is that the suggestion would be regarded as absurd, and probably regarded as absurd most strongly by those who are now most vociferous in dismissing the anti-Stratfordian case. This Stratford actor, it would be repeatedly asserted, had absolutely no qualifications to have written the

supremely literate and erudite works whose authorship is (in this case) unknown; it would be a reasonable and indeed near-certain inference that they must perforce have been written by a well-educated man, one familiar with Court life. Under these circumstances, anyone advocating William Shakespeare as the author of the plays would surely be dismissed as a crackpot.

13. Shakespeare's daughters and family – Shakespeare's two daughters were apparently illiterate, and could not read the works of their immortal father even if they wished to. Although the last of Shakespeare's immediate descendants died in 1670, descendants of his sister Joan Hart (née Shakespeare) survive to this day. None possesses, or has ever been known to possess, a book or scrap of paper owned by their illustrious ancestor. None of the 225 or so surviving copies of the First Folio of 1623 was ever known to have been owned by a member of Shakespeare's family (despite the fact that his widow and two married daughters were alive when it was being compiled), although the compilers of the First Folio would surely have, early on, inquired as to whether Shakespeare's family retained any unknown or revised manuscripts of his plays.

3

Edward de Vere
Seventeenth Earl of Oxford

Edward de Vere, seventeenth Earl of Oxford, was born on 12 April
1550 and died on 24 June 1604. He was thus fourteen years older
than William Shakespeare and died nearly twelve years before
Shakespeare's death, and nine years before the generally accepted
date of Shakespeare's last play. De Vere was the son of John de Vere,
sixteenth Earl of Oxford (1516–62) and his wife Margery, daughter
of Sir John Golding and the half-sister of Arthur Golding, the
translator of Ovid. Edward de Vere's education was slightly original:
he matriculated at Queens' College, Cambridge, in November 1558
at the age of eight and a half. His university career was brief, since he
remained there for one academic year. He was then tutored in the
household of Sir Thomas Smith by Thomas Fowle, a Master of Arts
of Cambridge University, who has been described by Alan Nelson
as 'a religious fanatic of violent temper'. After his father's death
in August 1562 (when de Vere was twelve), he succeeded to the
earldom and to the ceremonial office of Lord Great Chamberlain.★

★ The holder of this office presides at coronations and other major ceremonials. It should not be
confused with the position of the Lord Chamberlain, who was responsible, among other things,
for the Court's entertainment and for overseeing theatres. Shakespeare's acting company was
known as the Lord Chamberlain's Men from 1594 until 1663. This refers to the theatre supervisor,
not to the Lord Great Chamberlain.

He also became a ward of William Cecil (Lord Burghley), master of the Court of Wards. As Cecil's ward he was supervised by Lawrence Nowell, Dean of Lichfield, in French, Latin, penmanship, and dancing, and is known to have purchased books by Chaucer, Plutarch, and other authors. From 1567, however, he also exhibited another aspect of his character when, while practising fencing, he killed an unarmed cook. The coroner's jury absurdly found that the cook had committed suicide by 'running upon a point of a fence-sword' held by Oxford. Fifteen years later, Oxford fought a duel with Sir Thomas Knyvet, the uncle of his mistress Anne Vavasour (by whom he had an illegitimate son), and was seriously injured, with further vendettas lasting a year. As the ward of the very sympathetic Cecil, Oxford continually begged him for appointments and money, writing more than eighty letters to him, generally begging letters. In December 1571 he married Burghley's daughter Anne, in a marriage which was a spectacular failure, but produced four surviving daughters. Oxford was also a favourite of Queen Elizabeth, who particularly admired his skill at dancing. From 1574 to 1577 he made an extended trip to the Continent, visiting Paris, Strasbourg, Venice, Padua, Sienna, and Milan. On the Continent he also demonstrated his bisexuality, associating with both a Venetian choirboy and a Venetian courtesan, and became equally famous for his luxurious and often effeminate dress and tastes. On his return trip he managed to be robbed of his possessions by pirates in the English Channel. Back in England, he spent many years as a courtier, increasingly impoverished and forced to sell many of his estates, despite receiving an annuity of £1,000 per year – the equivalent of £1 million today – from the Queen from 1586 onwards. After the death of his first wife, in 1592 he married Elizabeth, daughter of Thomas Trentham, a squire in Staffordshire, by whom he had a son and heir. He died, probably of the plague, in July 1604, aged fifty-four, in his residence in Hackney, then still a semi-rural area. A Cecil loyalist, he opposed the Essex rebellion of 1601, and lived just long enough to oversee James I's coronation.

Oxford was an accomplished, if somewhat limited, poet, of whose poems at least sixteen survive. Most were apparently written early in Oxford's life. He was also well known in his lifetime as the author of plays, and in 1598 was termed 'the best for comedy' in Francis Meres' famous *Palladis Tamia* (which also named William Shakespeare and thirteen of his plays). None of Oxford's plays survive. Oxford, moreover, was the patron of an acting company, Oxford's Men, which existed from about 1580, when it took over the Earl of Warwick's Men, to about 1602, when it was absorbed by Worcester's Men. It performed at various places in London, but chiefly toured the provinces. Oxford also had a company of acting boys in the early 1580s. The names of only a few plays performed by Oxford's Men are known, none by Shakespeare, and none, according to the surviving records, by Oxford himself. He was also interested in music, and was the recipient of twenty-eight dedications of books and other works, including works by John Lyly and Anthony Munday (whom he employed), Edmund Spenser, and Thomas Watson.

Oxford thus appears to have been both talented and violent, brave and erratic, bisexual, artistic and, despite his ancient title, perpetually in need of money. He was a failure as a political intriguer and, indeed, arguably in almost everything he did. In the twentieth century he has been the subject of three deeply researched biographies: B.M. Ward's *The Seventeenth Earl of Oxford, 1550–1604, From Contemporary Documents* (1928); Alan Nelson's 527-page biography, *Monstrous Adversary: The Life of Edward de Vere, 17th Earl of Oxford* (2003), and Daphne Pearson's *Edward de Vere (1550–1604): The Crises and Consequences of Wardship* (2005), based upon her doctoral dissertation at Sheffield University, and using many original sources. Had it been left there, Oxford would be seen as an unusual, mildly interesting, aristocratic Elizabethan courtier, a good major-minor writer and theatre patron whose life might best be taken as illustrating Lawrence Stone's thesis that there was an 'economic crisis of the aristocracy' in late Elizabethan and Jacobean times which contributed to the eventual outbreak of the English Civil War nearly four decades after his death.

In 1920, however, there came a publication which fundamentally altered the perceptions which, agree with them or violently disagree, we have of de Vere: J. T. Looney's *'Shakespeare' Identified in Edward de Vere, Seventeenth Earl of Oxford*. John Thomas Looney (1870–1944) was a school teacher in Newcastle-upon-Tyne. He was familiar with the then-prevalent anti-Stratfordian theory that Sir Francis Bacon wrote the plays, but, dissatisfied with it, decided to approach the authorship question from a new angle, asking what personal characteristics the real author of Shakespeare's plays should reasonably have exhibited: in other words, what could reasonably be inferred from Shakespeare's works about the life of their author. Looney was convinced, as are many others, that the Stratford actor William Shakespeare could not have written the works attributed to him, and that the evidence of the plays and poems suggested quite a different man. Looney then drew up two lists of nine points each, which, he believed, were important characteristics of the real author. The first was a list of general aspects of the real Shakespeare:

1. A matured man of recognised status.
2. Apparently eccentric and mysterious.
3. Of intense sensibility – a man apart.
4. Unconventional.
5. Not adequately appreciated.
6. Of pronounced and known literary tastes.

7. An enthusiast in the world of drama.

8. A lyric poet of recognised talent.

9. Of superior education – classical – the habitual associate of educated people.

Whether or not Oxford was the real Shakespeare, it will surely be seen that this list, while it contains some good points, also enumerates some points which can be termed special pleading. The final point, 'of superior education', is reasonable enough, and a traditional and perfectly fair argument against the poorly educated Stratford man. Many of the other points are clearly less than that. Why, for instance, should the real author be 'a matured man'? Precisely the opposite seems more likely: the transcendent genius of the real author, whoever he was, would surely have produced plays from a young age. This point, moreover, takes no account of Shakespeare's evolution as a writer from his early plays, such as *Titus Andronicus*, to the great tragedies and after. In common with the rest of Looney's list, however, it does look suspiciously like he devised this criterion to fit Oxford, who was nearly forty when the first of Shakespeare's plays appeared. Other points made by Looney are also dubious. Why should the real author be 'apparently eccentric and mysterious'? What did Looney mean by 'eccentric'? Behaviour which might seem eccentric to a middle-class school teacher writing in 1920 might seem perfectly normal to Elizabethan aristocrats, let alone to writers and other habitués of London's *demi-monde* at the time. Moreover, that the real author is 'eccentric and mysterious' can plainly *not* be inferred from Shakespeare's works. If anything of this nature may be deduced from the pattern of authorship, it is surely that the real author was unusually businesslike, writing two plays each year or so in the first half of his career and one play each year or so in the second half of his career, with great regularity. Other points made by Looney are similar. How can he know that the author is 'not adequately appreciated'? What does this mean? William Shakespeare was reasonably well known in his lifetime, became wealthy from the theatre, and had a magnificent folio volume of his works produced shortly after his death, edited, it would seem, by the Poet Laureate. Were the real author was someone other than the Stratford man, he had only to make his actual identity known to the public to receive the appreciation which came to William Shakespeare.

Looney followed this with nine other special characteristics which the real author must have had:

1. A man with feudal connections.
2. A member of the higher aristocracy.
3. Connected with Lancastrian supporters.
4. An enthusiast for Italy.
5. A follower of sport (including falconry).
6. A lover of music.
7. Loose and improvident in money matters.
8. Doubtful and somewhat conflicting in his attitude toward women.
9. Of probable Catholic leanings, but touched with scepticism.

As before, this list contains some good points, such as the real author being 'an enthusiast for Italy', but also many very dubious ones. There is nothing in Shakespeare's work from which one might infer that he was 'a man with feudal connections' – whatever that might mean. England had not seen feudalism for perhaps 150 years when the plays were written. It had no serfs, no peasants, no private armies of noble retainers, but was noted for its ease of social mobility. The Tudor regime had centralised power in the Court/bureaucratic apparatus in London, based on Protestant patriotism and what Thomas Carlyle later called the 'cash nexus' of capitalism. There is absolutely nothing in Shakespeare's works from which anyone might infer that the author was 'a member of the higher aristocracy'. Shakespeare's triumphalist histories were largely based on the works of Edward Halle and Raphael Holinshed, two bourgeois, but emphatically pro-Tudor, writers. Shakespeare wrote in favour of political stability, but also in favour of the depositions and overthrowing of kings which brought the Tudors to power. In 1917, an American professor, Charles Mills Gayley, wrote *Shakespeare and the Founders of Liberty in America*, which saw the Bard, especially via his connections with the Jamestown expedition, as one of the remote progenitors of the United States and its republican government. Again, there is nothing in Shakespeare's works from which it might be concluded that he was 'loose and improvident in money matters'. William Shakespeare himself became a relatively wealthy man; his plays weren't copyrighted in the modern sense because they weren't owned by their author. That William Shakespeare was a secret Catholic has recently become a popular view, thanks to Shakespeare's alleged 'Lancashire connection', but his works, to reiterate, fully accept England's Protestant settlement, although they may use residual Catholic concepts such as that of Purgatory. It is, however, perfectly true that the author was 'doubtful and somewhat conflicting in his attitude toward women' – presumably a euphemism for being apparently bisexual. Shakespeare was, however, one of the first writers to create strong, non-stereotyped female characters, such as Portia and Lady Macbeth.

According to his own account, Looney then searched the *Dictionary of National Biography* and found Edward de Vere, the seventeenth Earl of Oxford, who appeared to exhibit all of these characteristics. As noted, it very much appears as if de Vere came first and the characteristics later, while, in any case, many of them are very dubiously ascribed to the Bard. Unsatisfied with either the likelihood that Shakespeare wrote the works attributed to him, or with the then-dominant alternative candidate, Sir Francis Bacon, Looney proposed and examined Oxford's case in a lengthy work.

While his methodology of inferring the real author's background from his works and then seeing who best fitted them has many merits, it is also the case that Looney's choice of characteristics omits many obvious major attributes of the true author. Most obviously, they fail to examine the dates of the real author and how this affects any accurate chronology of Shakespeare's works, a point which would almost automatically eliminate Oxford from serious consideration. Equally obviously, they do not include the real author's relations with the Lord Chamberlain's/King's Men, with Ben Jonson, or with the First Folio, and nor with the main political events of the time, especially the Essex rebellion of 1601. They are, in other words, highly selective and, it might be said, designed to point to Oxford as the real author, rather than being truly objective and helpful in the authorship debate.

Looney's work proved fruitful, and led, over the next few decades, to further publications by 'Oxfordians', as the supporters of the candidacy of the seventeenth Earl of Oxford are known. Early Oxfordians included Percy Allen, Eva Turner Clark, Charles Wisner Burrell, Montagu W. Douglas, Louis Benezet, and B.M. Ward, on both sides of the Atlantic. An unexpected, but most prestigious, convert to Oxfordianism was Sigmund Freud, who stated in a footnote in his last work, first published in German in 1940 as *Abriss der Psycho-Analyse* (and in English as *An Outline of Psychoanalysis*), that 'the name "William Shakespeare" is most probably a pseudonym behind which there lies a great unknown. Edward de Vere, Earl of Oxford, a man who has been regarded as the author of Shakespeare's works, lost a beloved, and admired father while he was still a boy, and completely repudiated his mother, who contracted a new marriage soon after her husband's death', thus bearing out the Oedipus complex seen by Freudians such as Ernest Jones as at the heart of *Hamlet*.

The Oxfordian movement then probably declined for some decades until the publication of *This Star of England: 'William Shake-spear', Man of the Renaissance* by Dorothy and Charlton Ogburn in 1952, and, more particularly, with the publication of *The Mysterious William Shakespeare*, a 1984 work by their son Charlton Ogburn Jr. The latter work, despite being 892 pages long, was only a *Reader's Digest* version of his parents' 1,297-page work. Ogburn Jr's work appeared in an inexpensive paperback edition, and possibly was a more important factor than any other in beginning the great revival of Oxfordianism which began about that time. Since then, probably several dozen pro-Oxfordian books have appeared, only some of which can be noted here. These include Richard Whalen, *Shakespeare – Who Was He: The Oxford Challenge to the Bard of Avon* (1994); Joseph Sobran, *Alias Shakespeare: Solving the Greatest Literary Mystery of All Time* (1997); Mark Anderson, *'Shake-Speare' By Another Name: The Life of Edward de Vere, Earl of Oxford* (2005), a lengthy biography; William Farina, *De Vere as Shakespeare: An Oxfordian Reading of the Canon* (2006); and the essays in Richard Malim, ed., *Great Oxford: Essays on the Life and Work of Edward de Vere, 17th Earl of Oxford, 1550–1604* (2004). Several very active pro-Oxfordian journals and societies exist, such as the well-produced *Shakespeare Oxford Newsletter*, published by the Shakespeare Oxford Society of Yorktown Heights, New York, and the *De Vere Society Newsletter*, published by the De Vere Society of Tunbridge Wells (of which Sir Derek Jacobi is a patron). Well-attended annual conferences are held at Concordia University in Portland,

Oregon, organised by Professor Daniel Wright, and there is also another pro-Oxfordian Shakespeare Authorship Conference held at Ashland, Oregon, in addition to annual conferences in England and in the Netherlands. The pro-Oxfordian movement appears stronger than ever, and has resulted in traditional pro-Stratfordians taking notice in an attempt to refute the anti-Stratfordian claims, especially those made by Oxford's adherents.

Points in Favour of Edward de Vere as the Real Shakespeare

A number of specific claims are consistently made by adherents of de Vere as Shakespeare, and it might be useful to examine and analyse these, followed by the points which are made against de Vere's candidacy as the true Bard:

1. Background and education – To a remarkable extent, Oxford had the right background, education, and experience to have written the plays. He was extremely well educated, multilingual, a traveller in Italy and elsewhere in Europe, a Court insider, and a man whose ancestors had been close to the centre of English power for centuries. Arthur Golding, the translator of Ovid, whose work was frequently used by Shakespeare, was his uncle. He was the son-in-law of Lord Burghley, widely seen as the model for Polonius in *Hamlet*. Given the erudition and classical learning in Shakespeare's plays, Oxford is an ideal candidate to have been the actual author.
2. Connections with the theatre and with poetry – Oxford was recognised in his time by Francis Meres as 'best for comedy' among playwrights, and, on the evidence of his few surviving

poems, was an accomplished poet. He was the patron of a long-existing acting company. He was thus a man close to the world of the Shakespearean theatre.

3. Parallels with Oxford's life in the plays – Oxfordians claim to see innumerable parallels drawn from Oxford's life in Shakespeare's plays. This is most strikingly the case in *Hamlet*, Shakespeare's most famous play. As in the play, Oxford's father died suddenly and his mother quickly remarried. He was the son-in-law of Lord Burghley. In the First Quarto (1603) of *Hamlet*, Polonius was named Corambis, which, Oxfordians point out, is a name plainly drawn from Burghley's motto *Cor unum, via una* ('One heart, one way'). Burghley was known for his sententious maxims, just like Polonius. In Act IV of the play, and à propos of nothing in particular, it is recorded that Hamlet was robbed by pirates, just as Oxford was on returning from Italy in 1575.

    These are also parallels in many other plays. The main character in *The Merchant of Venice* is Shylock, a name unknown to Italian Jews. In 1577, Oxford gave a bond of £3,000 to a London financier, Michael Lok (or Lock), which was never repaid. In the play, Antonio is in bond for 3,000 ducats pending the safe return of his ships. In *Henry IV Part I*, Falstaff and three friends rob travellers on the highway from Gravesend to Rochester. In 1573, in a letter written by two of Oxford's former employees to Lord Burghley, Oxford was accused of attacking them on the highway from Gravesend to Rochester. Throughout the history plays, the previous earls of Oxford are consistently given a greater role than they actually deserved. Many other such striking parallels have been noted by Oxfordians. These simply cannot be coincidences, it is claimed – there are simply too many of them, and their inclusion in the plays is often pointless unless they were autobiographical. Nothing in the known life of William Shakespeare can account for them.

4. Tell-tale events which indicate that de Vere was the real author – From 1586 Oxford was paid £1,000 a year by Queen Elizabeth, a sum which was renewed when James I came to the throne in 1603. This was an extraordinary sum, the equivalent of £1 million per year (tax-free) today. Apparently, the only Elizabethan official or courtier who was paid as much was the head of the Post Office. No one knows why Oxford was paid this remarkable sum; he was not given any official position to go with the salary, and had no obvious duties to perform for the money. Oxfordians argue that this was payment for writing the triumphalist history plays, later published under the pseudonym 'William Shakespeare'. At the Christmas Court Revels of 1604/05, a few months after Oxford died, eight Shakespeare plays were performed (as well as two by Ben Jonson and one, otherwise unknown, entitled *The Spanish Maze*, which Oxfordians argue was *The Tempest*). Oxfordians suggest that these performances were a memorial commemoration of Oxford's death. On 24 June 1604, the day Oxford died, King James arrested Lord Southampton, Sir Henry Neville (see below), Sir Maurice Berkeley, Lord Danvers, and Sir William Lee, all of whom had been connected with the Essex rebellion. Why they were arrested is a mystery, although King James apparently feared a coup of some kind. They were quickly released. Some Oxfordians believe that they had important information about Oxford's will (which has never been found), or possibly about his writings as 'Shakespeare'. Shakespeare knew that Giulio Romano, mentioned in *The Winter's Tale*, was a sculptor, described as 'that rare Italian master'. For many years, this was thought to be an error on Shakespeare's part, since Romano

was believed to have been a painter. More recently, it has become known that he was also a sculptor, and his works, in Mantua, must have been seen by the real author. Oxford is known to have visited Italy in 1575–76. Similarly, Shakespeare's detailed knowledge of the minute geography of northern Italy could only have been gained by an eyewitness such as Oxford. There is no evidence that William Shakespeare ever left England in his life. Another very interesting point is that the 1609 'second state' edition of *Troilus and Cressida* begins with an 'Epistle' to 'Eternall reader' by 'A never writer, to an ever reader'. Oxfordians claim that this is a teasing pun on Oxford's name, de Vere. The same 'Epistle' mysteriously states that the play was published 'by the grand possessors will', which Oxfordians argue is a reference to the holders of his posthumous manuscripts.

5. Parallels in the writings of Oxford and Shakespeare – Many Oxfordians believe that there are striking parallels in the writings of Oxford and Shakespeare, with similar imagery, vocabulary, metaphors, and the like. According to Oxfordians, these occur time and again, even in the limited number of poems by Oxford which survive, and simply cannot be coincidences. For instance, one of Oxford's poems begins:

> Ev'n as the wax doth melt, or dew consume away
> Before the sun, so I, behold, through careful thoughts decay.

This appears to be much like the lines in *Rape of Lucrece*:

> … as soon decay'd and done
> As is the morning's silver-melting dew
> Against the golden splendour of the sun!

Shakespeare's wording is obviously better and more sophisticated, but Oxford's poem might well be Shakespeare's juvenilia, as many Oxfordians argue.

6. Annotations in Oxford's Geneva Bible – Probably the closest thing to a 'smoking gun' possessed by Oxfordians are the handwritten annotations made in Oxford's own copy of the Geneva Bible (the translation produced in 1569–70). Now held at the Folger Library in Washington D.C., it contains 1,028 handwritten underlinings and marginal notes. In the 1990s, Dr Roger Stritmatter, a prominent Oxfordian, undertook a study of these annotations for his doctoral dissertation at the University of Massachusetts. He discovered that about one-fourth of the annotations appeared, either directly or in parallel, in Shakespeare's writings. Of eighty-one biblical verses used by Shakespeare four or more times, thirty were marked in Oxford's Bible. Some of these annotated verses were only identified for the first time as the sources of passages from Shakespeare because they could be traced from Oxford's annotations.

7. 'Our ever-living poet' – The famous Dedication of *Shakespeares Sonnets* mentions 'our ever-living poet', a phrase used exclusively, or almost exclusively, of someone who was dead. Oxford died in 1604, five years before the work's publication; all of the other major candidates (including William Shakespeare) were still alive in 1609.

8. Stratford and the Avon – Oxford lived his last years in Hackney, then a semi-rural suburb of London. Near to Hackney is Stratford, now a part of Greater London. Oxford owned an estate alongside the River Avon, near the Forest of Arden (the scene of part of *As You Like It*). Oxfordians claim that references to the author living at Stratford or near the Avon actually refer to Oxford, not Shakespeare.

Points Against Edward de Vere as the Real Shakespeare

Although Oxfordians since Looney have compiled a list of reasons why the seventeenth Earl of Oxford was the real author of Shakespeare's works, it is important to realise that there are many reasons to remain very sceptical. These include:

1. The lack of any real connection between Oxford and Shakespeare. While the Oxfordian theory has been known and discussed for more than nine decades, and has won over a fair number of adherents, many of whom have conducted their own primary research on the authorship question, not an iota of direct evidence has ever been found linking Oxford with Shakespeare, or with Shakespeare's circle, in any way, shape, or form. The Earl of Oxford left voluminous manuscripts behind, including letters and documents. He was a high-profile senior aristocrat, the subject of much popular and political gossip. Nothing – literally nothing – from contemporary sources links him in any way with William Shakespeare, Shakespeare's plays, Shakespeare's acting company, or Shakespeare's colleagues. The names of Shakespeare and Oxford are mentioned in the same document by a contemporary only once, in Francis Meres' celebrated *Palladis Tamia* of 1598, where (as noted) he states that Oxford as a playwright is 'the best for comedy', but then proceeds to name a long list of other accomplished writers of comedy, including 'Greene, Shakespeare, Thomas Nash' and so on. In other words, Meres thought that Oxford and Shakespeare were two different men. Oxford had no known connection with the Lord Chamberlain's/King's Men, Shakespeare's acting company. According to Oxford's biographer, Alan Nelson, in

his *Monstrous Adversary* (2003), 'Not only did Oxford have no demonstrable connection with the Lord Chamberlain's Men – Shakespeare's company – but neither the Carey family, the contemporary Lord Chamberlain, nor their successor patron King James, had any particular use for him.' Given the considerable research into every aspect of Oxford's life by his adherents in the decades since Looney's book appeared, it is rather remarkable that absolutely nothing linking Oxford and Shakespeare has ever been found by Oxfordians. After all this time, it is a reasonable inference that no connection between the two men will ever be found. Many Oxfordians say this was because Oxford wished to keep his identity as 'Shakespeare' a secret. But if the surprising lack of compelling evidence that William Shakespeare of Stratford was a playwright is taken as implying that he did not write the works attributed to him, it is obviously an example of blatant double standards to claim that the lack of sources linking Oxford and Shakespeare is actually evidence showing that Oxford wrote Shakespeare's works.

2. The wrong dates – For many sceptics about the case for Oxford, this is the most fundamental of all reasons to reject Oxford's 'candidacy'. Oxford was born in 1550 and died in 1604. Shakespeare's plays are universally taken to have been written between about 1588–90 – when Oxford was nearly forty – and 1613, nine years after his death. Several of Shakespeare's plays written after 1604 are universally taken to contain references to events after Oxford's death, especially *Macbeth* and, in particular, *The Tempest*, which was based in part on the Strachey Letter and other documents relating to the shipwreck at Bermuda in 1609. For Oxford to have written Shakespeare's works, the entire orthodox chronology of the works must be completely wrong, and

many of the plays must have been written well before their generally accepted date. Despite Oxfordian attempts to argue for a sweeping revision of the dates of Shakespeare's plays, they have persuaded no one who is not already a convinced Oxfordian. Moreover, Shakespeare's works demonstrate a clear evolutionary trajectory, with the Italianate comedies and triumphalist histories written before about 1601 – a great turning point in Shakespeare's outlook, for unknown reasons – and his great tragedies and the 'problem plays' written from about 1601 onwards. Oxfordians would have to demonstrate a similar credible pattern of development at an earlier date in a convincing way, which they have been unable to do.

3. Oxford had his own theatre company – This is an important point that is often overlooked. As we have seen, Oxford had his own theatre company which existed for many years, from about 1580 until 1603. Yet, after about 1594, all of Shakespeare's extant plays were performed by the Lord Chamberlain's/King's Men, with which he was associated. For instance, the title page of the First Quarto of *Hamlet* (1603) states that it was published 'as it hath beene diverse times acted by his Highest servants in the Cittie of London' – a reference to the King's Men, as Shakespeare's company was known after May 1603. If Oxford was the author of Shakespeare's works, why did he allow them to be performed by a rival theatre company with which he was not associated, the rival company presumably taking all of the admission revenues from the play's audiences? Oxford was in chronic need of money; surely putting on the Falstaff plays, or *Richard III*, or *Hamlet* would have eased his financial plight?

4. Oxford's surviving verse is nothing like Shakespeare's – Notwithstanding the claims outlined above that Oxford's surviving poems are similar to Shakespeare's, it must be

obvious to any intelligent reader that they are wholly unalike. Oxford's surviving poems lack all of the characteristic features of Shakespeare's, especially the complexity of meaning packed into a small space, the inventive use of metaphors, and the Bard's great originality in the use of new and rare words, among other well-known trademarks. Most of the alleged 'parallels' found by Oxfordians between his poetry and Shakespeare's are simply trite examples of the common usage of poetic ideas and imagery, and do not, on closer inspection, show any more in the way of real identity than would be expected of virtually any poet writing at the time. A comparison between Shakespeare and virtually any other well-known contemporary poet will also show similarities in phrasing and imagery.

Perhaps even more significantly, two American academics, Ward E.Y. Elliott and Robert Valenza, ran a sophisticated computer analysis of the writings of Shakespeare and twenty-six contemporary writers. None of those tested – which included most of the authorship candidates – was very close to Shakespeare. Oxford was particularly distant, showing a 'modal score' (a test of how often common words were used relative to each other) of 18.37 standard errors away from Shakespeare, ranking him twenty-second out of the twenty-six writers tested. Oxfordians naturally objected, protesting that Oxford's writings were his juvenilia and different in genre from the works of Shakespeare which were tested. In another test, Elliott and Valenza measured the use of feminine endings in blank verse, which increased steadily among English poets between the 1580s and the 1620s. This was clearly shown in a test of the writings of nineteen well-known contemporaries of Shakespeare, which revealed a sharp rise from around 1600 onwards. This pattern was also strikingly found in the plays of Shakespeare, when they were arranged in their normal chronological order. This tendency continued to increase at a steady rate among the plays written after 1604, the date of Oxford's death. In other words, the pattern of feminine endings was wholly consistent with the orthodox dating of Shakespeare's plays (*c.*1588/90–1613), but wholly inconsistent with a writer such as Oxford, who allegedly wrote Shakespeare's plays decades earlier than their generally accepted dating. Other studies of Oxford's idiosyncratic spelling have shown that this differed markedly from Shakespeare's. As to the marked passages in the Geneva Bible, apparently they were made by two different men – one of whom (at least) could not have been Oxford – while only about 10 per cent of Shakespeare's biblical allusions were marked in Oxford's Bible. Many of the books of the Bible most often drawn from in Shakespeare's works were hardly touched, while those parts most regularly marked were among those least often used by Shakespeare.

Many, probably most, of the alleged parallels between Oxford's life and plots or incidents in Shakespeare's plays also evaporate upon closer inspection. Although *Hamlet* is seen by most Oxfordians as closely drawn from Oxford's life, there are crucial differences. Unlike *Hamlet*, while it is true that Oxford's father died young and his mother remarried, his stepfather, Sir Charles Tyrrell, had not murdered Oxford's real father, and was not killed by Oxford. While Polonius might be a depiction of Lord Burghley, and Oxford was indeed married to his daughter, Oxford did not stab Burghley (but was a keen supporter of the Cecils), and Hamlet was not married to Ophelia. In any case, the plot of *Hamlet* was drawn from several well-known printed sources, such as Belleforest's *Histories Tragiques*, which contains the story of the King of Norway by the medieval Danish writer Saxo Grammaticus. The robbery at Gad's Hill in *Henry IV Part I* does indeed parallel an accusation made against Oxford by Lord Burghley's former employees, but was actually drawn from an anonymous 1594 play *Famous Victories of Henry V*, which was registered three or four years before Shakespeare's play, and has been described by all critics as lacking in skill and certainly not by Shakespeare.

5. Oxford had no relationship with Lord Southampton – Shakespeare dedicated *Venus and Adonis* (1593) and *Rape of Lucrece* (1594) to Henry Wriothesley, third Earl of Southampton (1573–1624). Most scholars believe that Southampton is also the dedicatee, as 'Mr. W. H.' (his initials reversed), of his *Sonnets* (1609). Southampton was imprisoned in the Tower for two years, 1601–03, for prominently supporting the Essex rebellion. Shakespeare's actual company, the Lord Chamberlain's Men, was known as the pro-Essex theatre, and famously produced Shakespeare's *Richard II* immediately before the uprising. Clearly, some close connection, over many years, existed between Southampton and Shakespeare – whoever he was – and his circle.

Oxford, however, had only the most marginal of relations with Southampton. They were both wards of Lord Burghley, but more than ten years apart. According to a Jesuit source (apparently our only source for this well-known allegation), in 1590 Southampton, Burghley's ward, paid a fine of £5,000 (an incredible sum) to *avoid* marrying Oxford's daughter. In 1601 Oxford served as the foreman of the jury of peers which tried Essex and Southampton for treason. Essex was executed, Southampton sent to the Tower. This represents the extent of connection between the two men; there is no reason to suppose that they ever met, or spoke, apart from official engagements and visits to the House of Lords. Over the Essex rebellion they were on opposite sides: Southampton was a key ally of Essex, Oxford a pro-Cecil super-loyalist.

6. Shakespeare's 'early' plays – In order to explain why no play by Shakespeare appeared until about 1590, many Oxfordian writers claim that plays from the 1570s or 1580s were actually written by Oxford, and are earlier versions of Shakespeare's plays, or identical to them. Thus, according to many Oxfordians, a play called *The Jew* (written *c.*1578–79) is actually an earlier version of *The Merchant of Venice*, normally dated to *c.*1596, and that *A Pastorall of Phyllida and Choryn* (1584) was actually *A Midsummer Night's Dream*, normally dated to *c.*1595. (None of these earlier plays survive in written form.) There is, however, not a shred of evidence that these early plays were related in any way to Shakespeare's plays, and there is not a shred of evidence that any of them was written by the Earl of Oxford. Oxfordians have to explain why Oxford did not write any of the works attributed to Shakespeare until he was forty or older, and are thus forced to draw unlikely conclusions about these earlier works. (For a sophisticated and useful attempt to create an Oxfordian chronology for his works, see Kevin Gilvary, ed., *Dating Shakespeare's Plays: A Critical Review of the Evidence* (2010).)

Another important point concerning Shakespeare's supposed early (pre-1590) plays is that no play now regarded as by Shakespeare was published prior to 1594, when *Titus Andronicus* appeared in quarto form. (A 'quarto' was a play published by itself, in contrast to the folio publication in 1623 of all of Shakespeare's plays.) If Oxford had actually written earlier versions of Shakespeare's plays, why were none published before 1594, when he was forty-four? The date of 1594 is plainly consistent with their having been written by a much younger author, whose earliest plays date from a few years before that date.

7. Oxford and the preparation of the First Folio – Oxford died in 1604; the First Folio, the great collection of Shakespeare's plays, did not appear until 1623, nineteen years later. If Oxford was the real author, where were the plays in the intervening period of nearly two decades? Why were they not published, as a tribute to Oxford, years earlier? Why were they suddenly published, out of the blue, nearly twenty years later? Of course, Oxfordians can give no convincing answer to any of these questions. Some, like Mark Anderson, suggest that they were published either as Protestant propaganda during the so-called Spanish Marriage Crisis of 1622–23 – when a marriage was being arranged between Prince Charles (later Charles I) and the Spanish princess, who was, of course, a Catholic – or in order to have the plays in print if an anti-Protestant Catholicism came to be the rule in England. But there is, of course, no evidence whatever for this. The prospective marriage fell through by September or October 1623, but the First Folio did not appear until November. It is difficult to see how Shakespeare's *complete* works (as opposed to his triumphalist histories) can be seen as Protestant propaganda, or how any marriage between the heir to the throne and a Catholic princess could possibly again bring to England the fearsome anti-Protestantism of seventy years earlier, given the entrenchment of Protestantism and the rise of extreme Puritanism. There is precisely no evidence that the publication of the First Folio had any religious or political motivations whatever. Moreover, Oxford's son and heir, Henry, the eighteenth Earl, was in the Tower of London during much of the period when the First Folio was being prepared. If Oxford was the actual author, presumably his

successor was the owner of the manuscripts and unpublished plays of 'Shakespeare'.

Summary

While Edward de Vere, seventeenth Earl of Oxford, may have had the background, education, and career of the actual author of Shakespeare's works, and was certainly a writer of note, not to mention the long-time patron of a theatre company, it seems evident that he was not the actual author. Indeed, given his dates of birth and death and lack of association with Shakespeare or his circle, he seems a rather implausible candidate. It is a genuine mystery why he is so popular as an alternative candidate, or why his popularity has risen so sharply in recent years. If this judgment is wrong, it is incumbent upon Oxford's many proponents to find real, convincing evidence for his candidacy as the real author.

Oxfordianism – Alternative Theories

In addition to the straightforward view that the seventeenth Earl of Oxford wrote Shakespeare's works, there are three other unorthodox theories about Oxford's role and background. These have won adherents although most Oxfordians regard them as (from their viewpoint) eccentric fringe theories.

The Oxford Group
The earliest variant of pure Oxfordianism was the group theory, that is, that Oxford acted as the leader of a group of leading playwrights and poets who, together, wrote Shakespeare's plays. (In variants of this theory, some other candidate, such as Sir

Francis Bacon, was the ringleader.) This theory apparently began in 1928, with B.M. Ward's biography of Oxford, but gained more prominence in 1931, in Gilbert Slater's *Seven Shakespeares: A Discussion of the Evidence for Various Theories with Regard to Shakespeare's Identity*, which puts forward the theory that the authorship of Shakespeare's works was organised by Oxford, but Bacon, Christopher Marlowe, William Stanley, Roger Manners, Sir Walter Raleigh, and the Countess of Pembroke, were co-authors. The entire operation, so the theory goes, was paid for by the government, Shakespeare's works being state propaganda. The 'group theory' had a long life and, until the recent strong revival of Oxfordianism, was one of the main ways in which Oxfordianism was viewed. For instance, in H.N. Gibson's 1962 study, *The Shakespeare Claimants*, the main chapter discussing de Vere is called 'The Case for the Oxford Syndicate'. Virtually all recent writers who view Oxford as the real author, however, believe that he wrote alone.

And well they might, for, needless to say, there is not a shred of evidence for this implausible theory. All of Shakespeare's works have the same 'voice', something implausible if not impossible if they were written by a group. To be sure, Shakespeare – whoever he was – did collaborate with other writers, for instance with John Fletcher on *Henry VIII*, but their respective portions of the play are clear to experts. The logistics of a group writing all of Shakespeare's works seem quite impossible, and even more impossible that it would leave no evidence or paper trail. If, say, Wagner, Tchaikovsky, Brahms, and Verdi collaborated on a symphony, each writing a single movement, apart from leaving a paper trail of evidence a mile long, the collaboration would surely be obvious to any trained musicologist, who would, surely, have no trouble in guessing the name of each composer.

1. One of only two apparently authentic portraits of William Shakespeare. This is the engraved portrait of Shakespeare on the title page of the First Folio (1623), by Martin Droeshout. It is, however, doubtful that Droeshout ever saw Shakespeare in life, and the picture is notorious for its amateurishness. The only other possibly authentic portrait of Shakespeare is the bust in Stratford church near his tomb, but its genuineness is open to doubt.

2. The earliest drawing of Shakespeare's monument in Stratford church, made by William Dugdale in 1653 and published in his *Antiquities of Warwickshire*. The man depicted here bears no resemblance to William Shakespeare as he appears on the monument today, and is resting his hands on what appears to be a sack of wool. Today, he is holding a quill pen over a cushion, while his appearance is completely different.

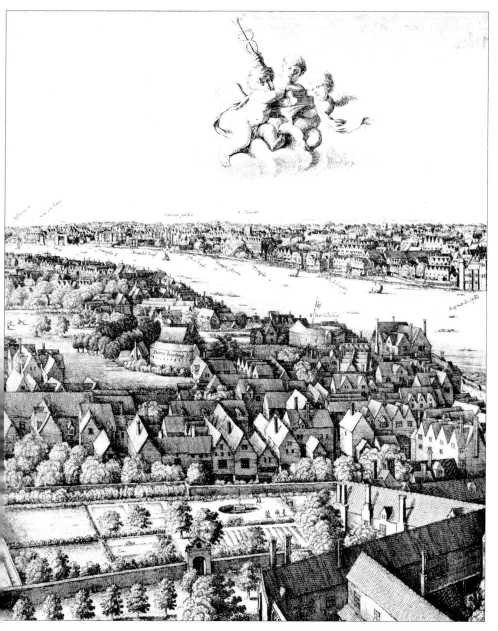

3. A view of the Bankside area of Southwark by Wenceslaus Hollar in 1647. The 'Bear-Bayting House' is actually the Globe Theatre.

4. The Globe Theatre, as depicted in 1616. It opened in 1599, burned down in 1613, and reopened the following year. Most of Shakespeare's later plays were performed here.

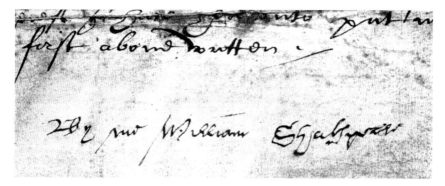

5a. The signature of William Shakespeare on his will, as dated 25 March 1616, one of only six known signatures of Shakespeare, all of which are on legal documents. The words before his signature, 'By me', are quite possibly the only surviving example of writing by Shakespeare apart from his signatures.

5b. Another signature of Shakespeare's, on a legal document of 1612.

Mʀ. WILLIAM
SHAKESPEARES

COMEDIES,
HISTORIES, &
TRAGEDIES.

Publiſhed according to the True Originall Copies.

LONDON

Printed by Iſaac Iaggard, and Ed. Blount. 1623.

6. The title page of the First Folio (1623), in which all of Shakespeare's plays were published for the first time. It appeared seven years after his death, and was probably edited by Ben Jonson, who wrote the famous poetic tribute to Shakespeare in the volume's introduction.

7. Edward de Vere, seventeenth Earl of Oxford (1550–1604). Today's leading authorship candidate, he was first proposed in 1920. Many societies, conferences, and journals exist today which promote him as the real Shakespeare.

8. Sir Francis Bacon (1561–1626). Unquestionably a man of multitalented genius, Bacon was the earliest alternative Shakespeare, first proposed in the early to mid nineteenth century.

9. William Stanley, sixth Earl of Derby (1561–1642). Another nobleman apparently well qualified to have been Shakespeare, Derby has his supporters today.

10. Sir Henry Neville (*c.*1562–1615). A recently discovered authorship candidate whose case appears stronger than that of any other candidate.

The 'Prince Tudor' Theory

A rather bizarre example of unorthodox history which has engendered an Oxfordian literature of its own is the so-called 'Prince Tudor' theory. This is the view that Oxford and Queen Elizabeth I were lovers, and Henry Wriothesley, third Earl of Southampton (Shakespeare's would-be patron), was their offspring. Another variant of the theory is that Oxford was actually the *son* of Queen Elizabeth by Thomas Seymour, Lord Admiral and the Queen's stepfather, conceived when she was fourteen. The first of these theories was first propounded in the 1920s. It was given support by the Ogburns in *This Star of England* (1953) and in recent works such as Hank Whittiemore's *The Monument* (2005). The second variant of the theory has been popularised in works such as Paul Streitz's *Oxford: Son of Queen Elizabeth I* (2001) and Charles Beauclerk's *Shakespeare's Lost Kingdom* (2010). (Beauclerk, a prominent Oxfordian, is a direct descendant of Oxford's.) It has recently become the basis of a film, *Anonymous*, released in 2011, which posits a theory of 'double incest', combining the two theories.

Both theories, of course, seem quite impossible, although the Queen may (or may not) have had lovers. It is virtually inconceivable that the existence of an illegitimate son of the Queen would be an impenetrable secret. His existence would be known to Lord Burghley, to most Court insiders, to foreign diplomats stationed in London (who made a point of learning every iota of gossip), and to friends of friends. Any son of the Queen would be a *prima facie* candidate to become the new monarch after her death, and would assuredly have had many champions among the aristocracy, the gentry, and other important interests, who would prefer his succession to that of the unknown Scotsman James I (James VI of Scotland), who had never previously set foot in England. Neither Oxford nor

Southampton would have been allowed to succeed to their titles and family property if there had been any doubts that they were the rightful heirs of their fathers. It is also inconceivable that historians would not by this time have learned of any illegitimate child of Queen Elizabeth, after pouring through the thousands of documents and letters which survive from the Elizabethan age.

Even if Queen Elizabeth had had an illegitimate son, it is even more improbable that he would have been the real author of Shakespeare's works, that is, the works of the greatest writer in history. The odds against this are obviously astronomical. No one imagines that Charles I was the real father of Sir Isaac Newton, or George IV of Charles Darwin or Charles Dickens: many English monarchs down the ages have fathered illegitimate children, but probably none has grown up to become a leading intellectual or cultural figure. Moreover, the Lord Chamberlain's Men, Shakespeare's acting company, was strongly associated with the pro-Essex, anti-Cecil and anti-Elizabeth forces during the rebellion of 1601.

Shakespeare Plus

Just when you might think that Oxfordian theories could not become more *outré*, one discovers that the limits have not yet been reached. There is a persistent school of thought at the fringes of Oxfordianism which argues that the earl not only wrote his own works and those of William Shakespeare, but many other books and literary works normally attributed to other authors. This notion apparently began with the early Oxfordian Eva Turner Clark, writing in 1930, who attributed twenty plays to Oxford between 1577 (when he was seventeen) and 1585, the earliest being *A Historie of Error* (presumably the original of *A Comedy of Errors*), *The Historie of the Solitarie Knight*, and *The Historie of*

Titus and Gisippus, all from early 1577. According to Paul Streitz, writing in *Oxford: Son of Queen Elizabeth I* (2001), even this does not do justice to Oxford's precocious genius, his earliest works all being written in 1562 (when Oxford was either eleven or twelve): *Jack the Juggler* (a play), *Romeus* [*sic*] *and Juliet*, a poem attributed to Arthur Brooke, and *Spinning Wheel Poem*. By 1564–66 he had produced translations of Julius Caesar, Ovid, and Seneca, and had also written *Ralph Roister Doister*, universally attributed to Nicholas Udall. He also wrote works usually attributed to John Lyly, Thomas Kyd, and Christopher Marlowe. 'Edward de Vere produced an almost unimaginable stream of poems, translations, essays, songs, and plays of the highest literary quality throughout every year of his life,' Streitz claims.

Even *this*, however, is not enough for Michael Brame and Galina Popova, who claimed, in their *Shakespeare's Fingerprints* (2002), that Oxford wrote all of the English literature produced in his time, including the works of Spencer and Marlowe. According to them, he began at the age of *eight* by translating Virgil's *Aeneid*, a translation usually ascribed to Thomas Phaer. Oxfordian Paul H. Altrocchi is somewhat more moderate, accepting that de Vere was the actual translator of Ovid's *Metamorphoses*, usually ascribed to Arthur Golding, at the relatively late age of fifteen, with a second instalment produced at seventeen. 'The poet [Oxford] not only metamorphosed 12,000 of Ovid's lines into inspired poetry … but also added 2500 new lines and invented dozens of new words' (Paul H. Altrocchi, 'Searching for Shakespeare's Earliest Published Works', *Shakespeare Oxford Newsletter*, May 2010). According to Paul Streitz ('Oxford and the King James Bible', *Shakespeare Matters*, Spring 2011, a leading Oxfordian journal), Oxford was the actual translator/editor of the King James Bible – the standard English-language edition for the past four centuries – not the fifty-four scholars, working in six committees in Cambridge, Oxford, and Westminster, to whom the translation is normally attributed. There would appear to be a minor flaw in his argument, since Oxford died in June 1604, while King James I did not authorise the translation until the following month, work on the project did not begin until 1607, and the Bible was not published until 1611. Oxford's death is recorded in the parish registers of St Augustine's church in Hackney (then a semi-rural area, where Oxford owned a mansion) in the same manner as hundreds of other entries. No, says Streitz, Oxford actually survived until 1607 or 1608, spending his time editing the Bible, as well, one supposes, as writing more of Shakespeare's plays. There is no real evidence that Oxford knew Hebrew, but never mind.

It was certainly rather selfish of Oxford not to leave *some* literary works to be written by someone else. One is also puzzled why this transcendent genius limited his creativity merely to literature, and did not also discover, for instance, the circulation of the blood normally attributed to William Harvey, or the rings of Saturn and moons of Jupiter which Galileo is said to have discovered, or why he did not anticipate the discovery of calculus by Newton and Leibnitz. It is just possible, one imagines, that the Earl of Oxford did write Spenser's *The Faerie Queene*. What is much more doubtful is that he wrote *Hamlet*.

4

Sir Francis Bacon

Sir Francis Bacon (1561–1626), later Lord Verulam and then Viscount St Albans, was unquestionably one of the greatest men of his age. He was the son of Sir Nicholas Bacon, the Lord Keeper of the Seal, and his mother, Anne Cooke, was the sister of Lord Burghley's wife (and also the sister of Sir Henry Neville's stepmother). He was educated by private tutors and then at Trinity College, Cambridge, where he became profoundly learned in Latin and medieval humanism, and then became a barrister at Gray's Inn. He spent over two years in France, accompanying the English ambassador, becoming fluent in French. An impecunious younger son after his father's death in 1579, he made his way, at first very slowly, as a barrister and Member of Parliament. Bacon's career is arguably unique in combining a job as a barrister and public official – in which, until his impeachment in 1621, he was remarkably successful – and a role as a philosopher of international importance. His career flourished, in particular, in the early part of King James I's reign, as he became Solicitor General in 1607, Attorney General in 1613, Lord Keeper in 1618, and Lord Chancellor from 1618 to 1621, also receiving a peerage. He is better known today as the author of such works as *The Advancement of Learning* (1605) and

New Atlantis (1627), in which he argued that empirical, scientific knowledge was superior to accepting classical learning at face value, and that science and technology should be used for the improvement of mankind. In 1621, at the height of his career, he was impeached and removed from office for corruption, a charge in part true, but greatly exaggerated by his numerous political enemies. He never held office again. Bacon was without doubt a most remarkable man, with an extraordinary record. The printout of his entry in the recent *Oxford Dictionary of National Biography* is forty-eight pages long, one of the longest entries in this standard work of reference. Many biographers have noted the apparent contradiction between his own career, which was often self-seeking and Machiavellian, and in which he supported England's continuing military might, and the international utopianism of his philosophical and scientific ideas. Bacon is also something of an enigma in his private life. In 1606, aged forty-five and a bachelor, he married a fourteen-year-old girl, Alice Barnham, whom he subsequently cut out of his will, apparently for adultery. Bacon was frequently accused of being a homosexual paedophile, a claim accepted by recent biographers.

Whether Bacon wrote poetry or literary works, that is, apart from his legal and philosophical works, is also somewhat debatable. Bacon wrote what might be termed some poems in the form of his *Translations of Certain Psalms into English Verse* (1624), and may have written a number of other poems as well. In the theatre, he was involved in writing the Gray's Inn Christmas Rounds of 1594/95, and at least one masque, written for the Court, in 1613, as well as a number of other quasi-theatrical ventures. But he had no known direct role with any acting company and was certainly not known as a literary writer like Marlowe or even Oxford. Nevertheless, when questions arose about the actual author of Shakespeare's works in the early to mid nineteenth century, it was Sir Francis Bacon who immediately became the earliest (and, for many years, the only) alternative candidate. Bacon essentially had the field to himself until the First World War or even after. For many decades, indeed, the anti-Stratfordian movement was widely known as the 'Baconian heresy'. In recent years, with the ascendancy of the Oxfordian movement and the championing of other possible candidates, less has been heard of Baconianism. Some pro-Baconian books do continue to be published, for instance N.B. Cockburn's *The Bacon Shakespeare Question: The Baconian Theory Made Sane* (1998), an excellent and very comprehensive work, and Peter Dawkins's deeply researched *The Shakespeare Enigma* (2004), and the theory still has many high-profile adherents, for example Mark Rylance, the actor and former head of the Globe Theatre. At least two pro-Bacon societies still exist, in Claremont, California, and Islington, London.

Points in Favour of Sir Francis Bacon as the Real Shakespeare

1. He was unquestionably a man of great learning and genius – If Shakespeare was undoubtedly a supreme genius among playwrights and poets, Sir Francis Bacon was surely his equal as a thinker and philosopher. Whoever wrote Shakespeare's works must have been a man of the highest intelligence, and few (if any) contemporaries of Shakespeare could even begin to equal Bacon's genius.
2. His background and career were appropriate for the actual author – Highly educated, a Member of Parliament, a senior office holder, a man who rubbed shoulders with the highest in the land, yet was also a philosopher, a linguist, and a

voracious reader, Sir Francis Bacon was, again, one of the few whose background, education, and career made him capable of writing Shakespeare's works.

3. His dates are right – Unlike the Earl of Oxford, Sir Francis Bacon's dates are consistent with the standard chronology of Shakespeare's works. Bacon was born in 1561, and would thus have been about twenty-seven or so when the first Shakespeare plays were written. He died in 1626, thirteen years after the last Shakespeare play was written, but pro-Baconians argue that, after 1613, Bacon was simply too busy to write plays. They also claim that his impeachment in 1621 led directly to the compilation and editing of the First Folio, as well as to his retirement from writing plays.

4. Bacon was the original candidate – Sir Francis Bacon was the earliest alternative candidate proposed as the real Shakespeare, and for seventy years was virtually the only one; he continued to be the leading candidate for another generation after that. This does not prove that he was actually William Shakespeare. But many excellent scholars and researchers of that period, men and women well versed in every aspect of Shakespeare's life and works, turned initially to Bacon as the most plausible real author. They surely knew what they were doing.

5. Shakespeare was learned in the law – Innumerable lawyers, judges, and legal experts during the past two hundred years have stated that Shakespeare had an expert and very precise knowledge of English law, and must surely have had legal training. Shakespeare often used legal phrases and quoted effortlessly from legal cases – or so the argument goes. Once again, Sir Francis Bacon, one of the greatest lawyers in England and Lord Chancellor, seems manifestly qualified to have written Shakespeare's works, far more so than any alternative authorship candidate.

6. Bacon's connections with Shakespeare – There are a number of times and places at which Bacon and Shakespeare seemed to mix, or perhaps mesh. Most strikingly, the revels produced at Gray's Inn over Christmas in 1594/95, attributed by even orthodox biographers to Bacon, accompanied a performance of Shakespeare's *The Comedy of Errors*. The revels and the play resulted in a drunken semi-riot known as 'the night of errors'. Moreover, the Chamber Accounts show that on that night Shakespeare's company, the Lord Chamberlain's Men, were actually at Greenwich, performing before the Queen. Bacon was also a friend of the Earl of Essex and of Lord Southampton, although he broke with them at the time of the Essex rebellion. Bacon later resumed his friendship with Southampton, and served on the council of the London Virginia Company with him.

7. Bacon's *Promus* – Bacon wrote a lengthy series of manuscript notes, published in 1883 as *The Promus of Formularies and Elegances* ('Promus' means 'storehouse'). This is a notebook or commonplace book of biblical texts, pithy sayings, and phrases from foreign languages, apparently written in 1594/95, and now at the British Library. The *Promus* contains about 1,655 entries, and some Baconians claim that over 1,400 of these can be traced in Shakespeare's works, often word for word. Another Baconian estimate, probably more realistic, is that about 600 of the *Promus* entries can be found in Shakespeare's works. Even pro-Stratfordian authors accept that there are many striking parallels. *Romeo and Juliet* (published in 1597, but certainly written earlier) appears to contain more parallels than any other play. Stratfordians either pass over the *Promus* in silence (the usual strategy), or claim that the use of these pithy sayings by two authors who were exact contemporaries is simply a coincidence;

moreover, most of the *Promus* sayings are not found in Shakespeare.

8. The St Albans mural – In 1985 (as recently as that) workmen renovating an old inn found an old wall-painting behind more recent panelling. It proved to be a picture of the hunt scene in *Venus and Adonis*, Shakespeare's long poem of 1593. The panel was found, of all places, in the White Hart Hotel (built in the 1300s) in St Albans, Hertfordshire, where Bacon had his country house and from which he took his peerage title. Baconians were not slow to point out that if this same panel had been found in an old tavern in or near Stratford-upon-Avon, its existence would assuredly be shouted from the rooftops as proof positive that Shakespeare of Stratford was the actual author of *Venus and Adonis*. Most Stratfordians have dismissed the existence of the panel as a coincidence, or ignored it. Curiously, no similar panel has ever been found in or near Stratford-upon-Avon to commemorate its greatest son's early work (or any other).

9. The Northumberland Manuscript – In 1867 twenty-two old manuscript sheets were discovered at Northumberland House at Charing Cross in London, the London mansion of the dukes of Northumberland. The top cover contained innumerable scribblings which appeared to show the contents which the bundle once contained. It *appears* that the scribblings may have been in Bacon's hand, although this is unclear. The importance of the Northumberland Manuscript is that, most remarkably, it contains the words 'By Mr Francis Bacon' and 'William Shakespeare' (written many times), as well as the names of the Shakespearean plays 'Richard the Second' and 'Richard the Third'. The manuscript also contains many other names, headed by 'Neville' and including 'by Thomas Nashe', 'Earle of Arundell's letter

to the Queen', 'Speaches for my Lord of Essex at the tylt', 'Asmund and Cornelia', and 'Ile of Dogs', among others. The 'Speaches for my Lord of Essex at the tylt' are thought to have been written by Bacon in 1596. The page on which all this is written appears to have been specifically designed to hold manuscripts rather than printed works, which makes the references to two Shakespeare plays more intriguing. The manuscript also mysteriously contains the word 'honorificab-ilitudinitatibus', used once by Shakespeare in *Love's Labour's Lost*, Act V, Scene 1, line 39.

Everything about this strange sheet of paper is most curious, and there is really no good explanation as to why it was penned or what its real purpose was. The association of the names of Bacon and Shakespeare on the sheet is certainly remarkable, and the sheet has, naturally, been regularly used by Baconian theorists. The name 'Nevill' on the top of the sheet is also significant, and may also point to Sir Henry Neville as the author (q.v.).

10. Labeo – Joseph Hall (1574–1616) wrote two volumes of satires entitled *Virgidemiarum*. In the second volume (1598) he attacked a writer he named 'Labeo' for writing erotic poetry and scenes of drunken revelry, and the work contains an apparent reference to *Venus and Adonis*. Another contemporary satirist, John Marston (*c.*1675–1634) addressed Hall with the words, 'What, not *mediocris firma* from thy spite?', an apparent reference to Bacon's family motto, *Mediocris firma* ('Hold fast to the middle course'). It is not just Baconians who have argued that this is a clear reference to Bacon having written *Venus and Adonis*. All of this is rather cryptic, as are so many references from Elizabethan literary works, but they appear to point to Bacon.

11. The 'great instauration' – Bacon's long-term philosophical project was one he termed the 'great instauration', the investigation of nature by direct observation, that is, the methodology of modern science. But, although Bacon was conscious of human psychology as a major field of study, he never wrote much about it. Baconians argue that he did, in the form of Shakespeare's plays, which famously take all human life and activity as their subject, and are animated by a universal humanism.

Points Against Sir Francis Bacon as the Real Shakespeare

1. Bacon's prose style – Sir Francis Bacon's elephantine prose style is utterly unlike Shakespeare's, and stands in comparison with Shakespeare's style in roughly the same way that the poems of Pushkin compare to a speech by Leonid Brezhnev on tractor production in the Urals. Unless Bacon totally changed his style when he assumed the role of 'Shakespeare', he could not have written Shakespeare's works.

2. The lack of any connection between Bacon and Shakespeare – Apart from the few possible strands outlined above which might connect Bacon and Shakespeare, there is really nothing whatever to associate the two men. Bacon had no known linkage with the Lord Chamberlain's/King's Men, or with Shakespeare's known circle of friends and associates. He was one of the most visible and controversial public men of his day, and one who left a considerable body of his own writings. But no paper trail of any kind exists connecting the two men. Apart from the revels and masques noted above, Bacon had no known connection with the London theatre.

3. Bacon and Italy – One major prop of anti-Stratfordians is that the real author, whoever he was, must have visited Italy, since he apparently had a profound knowledge of the local geography of many places there. William Shakespeare of Stratford almost certainly never visited Italy – there is absolutely no evidence that he did. But nor did Francis Bacon. According to his entry in the *Oxford Dictionary of National Biography*, around 1577, when he was in France, 'he planned a trip to Italy but [the English ambassador, Sir Amias] Paulet did not grant him permission, mainly on religious grounds'.

4. Bacon and Essex – Shakespeare's theatre company, the Lord Chamberlain's Men, was known as the pro-Essex theatre group in the period before the Essex rebellion, and performed *Richard II* immediately prior to the uprising. Although Bacon was a friend and admirer of Essex in the 1590s (mainly, it seems, because he thought Essex could help his career), Bacon was a major prosecutor of Essex and his followers at their trials once the rebellion petered out. Of course, if he were the actual author of *Richard II*, he would have bent over backwards to appear loyal to the Queen and Cecil, but one of his enemies, or Essex himself, might have been expected to point out that he was also 'William Shakespeare'.

5. Bacon and the Secret Codes – Baconianism was discredited by the early twentieth century namely because of the attempts by many Baconians to find secret codes or ciphers in Shakespeare's works which 'prove' that Bacon was the real author. Bacon was, moreover, well aware of secret codes, and wrote about them in the context of 'wheel ciphers; key ciphers, word ciphers' (in his *De Augmentis Scientiarum* of 1623) and other devices used chiefly in diplomacy. Nineteenth-century Baconians, most notoriously Ignatius Donnelly (1831–1901), spent decades trying to find encoded

evidence in Shakespeare's works proving that Bacon was the real author, surely one of the greatest wastes of time in literary history. (Donnelly was a famous radical American politician who wrote the eloquent platform of the People's Party (the Populists) of 1892, but was also known as the 'king of cranks', producing the first modern book on Atlantis and various 'funny money' currency theories.) The long and wholly pointless association of Baconianism with secret codes probably did more than anything else to discredit not merely Baconianism but all anti-Stratfordianism as a serious enterprise. There are contemporary variants of this kind of fringe theorising in, for instance, attempts to link Bacon with the Rosicrucians, a kind of forerunner of the Freemasons, as being behind the plays and their alleged symbolism and deeper meanings.

6. Bacon was a very busy man – Throughout his career, Sir Francis Bacon must have been one of the busiest men in England, with an extraordinarily full career as a barrister, court official, courtier, Lord Chancellor, and, as well, a major and much-published philosopher. That he also wrote thirty-seven plays, two long poems, and over 150 shorter ones, using the pseudonym of an actor, seems highly implausible, especially as Shakespeare's plays appeared at regular, reliable intervals – around two per year before 1601, and one per year or so after that. If Bacon were the real author, he would also have needed a means of conveyance of his plays to the theatre, copyists and scribes to produce the 'foul papers', an apparatus to proofread and correct the quartos, and so on. It seems improbable that there is no evidence for any of this.

7. The evolutionary trajectory of the plays – As has been noted several times, Shakespeare's plays have a clear evolutionary trajectory, with the Italianate comedies and triumphalist

histories written before 1601, the great tragedies and the 'problem plays' after that, before closure in *The Tempest*. Little or nothing in Bacon's life is really in accord with this. Indeed, if Bacon was the real author, the plays appear to have been written in the wrong order: Bacon's career flourished under James I, not before, and he should have written the comedies and histories after 1603, not well before.

8. The first and second person – In her *The Bacon Shakespeare Question,* Charlotte Carmichael Stopes (who thought that Shakespeare wrote the plays, not Bacon) pointed out that Bacon wrote many of his works in the first person, using 'I' about his thoughts and beliefs. In contrast, Shakespeare never wrote in the first person, even when expressing even his own thoughts in the sonnets. Of course, the characters in his plays spoke in the first person, but as entirely separate and individual men and women.

5

Christopher Marlowe

One of the strangest of authorship candidates is Christopher Marlowe. This is not because of his intellectual qualifications to be the real Bard, which are very great, but because he definitely died on 30 May 1593, stabbed to death at Deptford Strand near London, at the age of about twenty-nine. In 1593 the great majority of Shakespeare's plays had yet to be written, and with such an early death there can be no conceivable fudging of the chronology of Shakespeare's works, as proponents of the candidacy of the Earl of Oxford, who died in 1604, are fond of doing. For Marlowe to have been the real author, his murder must therefore necessarily have been a fake and he must necessarily have survived. Most Marlovians – as his proponents are known – believe that he fled either to France or to northern Italy, where he continued to write the plays attributed to Shakespeare, presumably actually dying around the same time as the Stratford man.

Christopher Marlowe (whose name was sometimes spelled 'Marley' and in other ways) was baptised in Canterbury, Kent, on 26 February 1564, two months before William Shakespeare at Stratford, making them exact contemporaries. His father, John Marlowe (*c.*1536–1605) was a shoemaker and warden of the local

Shoemaker's Company, rather like Shakespeare's father. He was educated as a scholar of the King's School, Canterbury, the oldest surviving English 'public school', where he received an unusually good education, and proceeded to Corpus Christi College, Cambridge, again as a scholar, although his career there was undistinguished academically. Marlowe had already developed a reputation for violent affrays and the questioning of authority, and had apparently already written some of his earliest works. He was also probably employed on the European continent on what would now be termed 'intelligence service' for Sir Francis Walsingham in 1585–87 but returned to London in 1587, and began to write his great plays, starting with *Tamburlaine the Great* (*c.*1587), followed by *The Jew of Malta* (*c.*1592), *Doctor Faustus* and *Edward II* (*c.*1592). He also produced poems and translations, and was twice involved in brawls with legal consequences. His end came, as noted, in May 1593 at a tavern in Deptford, where he was accompanied by three other men, one of whom, Ingram Frizer, stabbed and killed him. Frizer was a servant of Walsingham's, and the others were also involved in the murky and dangerous world of Elizabethan espionage. Marlowe had also repeatedly been accused of atheism and blasphemy, and was apparently notorious for his alleged beliefs. It should also be noted that Marlowe's plays were performed by the Lord Admiral's Men or by Lord Strange's acting company, not by the Lord Chamberlain's Men (Shakespeare's acting company), which was not formed until 1594 and did not subsequently perform Marlowe's plays. Indeed, there are no known direct links between Marlowe and Shakespeare. But Shakespeare clearly based some of his early plays on Marlovian forms, and appears to quote a line from Marlowe's poem *Hero and Leander* in *As You Like It*.

Marlowe's murder was quickly followed by an official inquest, discovered by the noted Shakespearean scholar Leslie Hotson in

1925, which claimed a fight had broken out over paying the bill, '*le reckynge*' in French, and that Marlowe initiated the fight. (Some writers have not realised that *le reckynge* refers to the tavern bill, not to some kind of 'reckoning' with Marlowe's life and fate.) Many mainstream scholars have questioned the full accuracy of the inquest account, given the connection of the men with the murky world of espionage, but the fact that it was both formal and official, as well as no different from any other inquest of its kind, and concerned a victim with a known record of violence, strongly implies that it is genuine and should be taken at face value. Marlowe was buried on 1 June 1593 at St Nicholas's church, Deptford, and received many poetic tributes. As has been repeatedly noted, had Shakespeare – whoever he was – died in 1593, and Marlowe lived on, Marlowe rather than Shakespeare would be universally regarded as the better writer.

Attempts to somehow link Marlowe with Shakespeare began surprisingly early. Edmund Malone, whose edition of Shakespeare appeared in 1790, thought that Marlowe had written *Titus Andronicus*, and many mainstream commentators, including Sir Sidney Lee in his entry on Marlowe in the old *Dictionary of National Biography*, thought that Marlowe might have written parts of Shakespeare's early plays. Indeed, in some respects they were the first mainstream 'anti-Stratfordians' although naturally they did not claim for Marlowe any works written after 1593. (It is interesting to note that the entry on Marlowe in the recent *Oxford Dictionary of National Biography*, by Charles Nicholl, makes no such claims.) In 1901 the American physicist Dr Thomas Mendenhall compared, in a primitive but comprehensive way, the pattern of word lengths in the works of Shakespeare and some of his contemporaries, especially Bacon, the leading alternative candidate at the time. As a comparison, he also included the works of Marlowe. Mendenhall found that while Bacon compared poorly with Shakespeare, Marlowe's word lengths were almost precisely identical to Shakespeare's. This method is, of course, highly problematical, if for no other reason than the same words were spelled in different ways in Shakespeare's works. Many years later, this was followed by the best-known Marlovian work, Calvin Hoffman's *The Man Who Was Shakespeare* (known in America as a *The Murder of the Man Who Was Shakespeare*), published in 1955. Hoffman argued that the account of Marlowe's murder was a sham, and that Marlowe survived, presumably on the European continent. Hoffman achieved considerable prominence by his success in opening the grave of Sir Thomas Walsingham (d. 1630), where he believed Shakespeare's manuscripts, actually written by Marlowe, were hidden. The grave was indeed opened in 1956; nothing was found.

There is still an active Marlovian movement, which has seen the publication of a number of pro-Marlovian works in recent years, such as Simon Blumenfeld, *The Shakespeare–Marlowe Connection: A New Study of the Authorship Question* (2008) and Daryl Pinksen, *Marlowe's Ghost: The Blacklisting of the Man Who Was Shakespeare* (2008). There is a Marlowe Society and an International Marlowe Society, both of which have websites.

Points in Favour of Christopher Marlowe as the Real Shakespeare

1. He was unquestionably a great writer – Marlowe is the only authorship candidate of whom this may be said, without qualification. Oxford was apparently a good comic playwright, and a fairly good poet. Bacon was a great philosopher and legal writer. Yet Marlowe alone wrote dramatic masterpieces

which, at the point of his alleged death in 1593, were better than Shakespeare's, and dealt with much the same subject matter as in the plays of Shakespeare.

2. Marlowe was well qualified to write the plays – By his excellent education, his government connections, and his direct participation in the London theatre world, Marlowe was exceedingly well qualified to have written Shakespeare's works. Again, this combination of qualifications is very rare. Marlowe also certainly travelled in France and by birth was a precise contemporary of the Stratford man.

3. There is an apparent mystery about his death – Over many generations, Marlowe's apparently pointless killing over a tavern bill has attracted considerable scepticism. Even many mainstream commentators believe that there was more to this than meets the eye, especially given the involvement of those present in secret government intelligence activities. The assumption that Marlowe actually survived his 'death' does not necessarily involve any leaps of fantasy.

4. He wrote like Shakespeare – As Mendenhall was the first to point out, Marlowe's dramatic works appear to sound much like Shakespeare, not merely in their word length but their soaring eloquence and general format.

5. Exit Marlowe, enter Shakespeare – None of the earliest quarto publications of Shakespeare's plays have his name on the title page; his name only appears after Marlowe's alleged death. According to Marlovians this is a more reasonable scenario for any use of 'William Shakespeare' as a pseudonym. All of the other authorship candidates would have had to have made use of 'William Shakespeare' as a pseudonym in their own active lifetimes. With Marlowe's alleged death and flight abroad, however, and given his work for England's intelligence service, it was perfectly reasonable for him to

use the living actor Shakespeare as a frontman. One must, however, be careful here. Shakespeare's poem *Venus and Adonis* was entered in the Stationer's Register, with William Shakespeare given as the author, in April 1593, a month before Marlowe's apparent death in May 1593. Marlovians would no doubt claim that his 'death' was already being planned, and the sudden appearance of a poem by 'William Shakespeare' was also pre-planned.

Points Against Christopher Marlowe as the Real Shakespeare

1. Marlowe died in 1593 – Despite many attempts to make Marlowe's death seem mysterious and possibly fraudulent, there seems not the slightest doubt, from contemporary documents discovered centuries after the event, that he died in 1593. He therefore could not have written any of Shakespeare's works produced after that date – no fewer than about thirty-one plays.

2. Marlowe's style is not Shakespeare's – While Marlowe was unquestionably a great playwright, he was also a less subtle and rather nastier one, lacking Shakespeare's universal humanism and ability to empathise with all of his characters. He also lacked many other typical qualities of Shakespeare's works, for instance his frequent invention of new words.

3. Marlowe and Shakespeare were (briefly) writing at the same time – Marlowe's own plays were attributed to him during his lifetime. Even if he later somehow wrote *Hamlet* and *Macbeth*, he did not also write Shakespeare's earliest plays such as the *Henry VI* trilogy and *Richard III*, written in Marlowe's lifetime. If he did, why were they not attributed to him?

4. There is no evidence for Marlowe's survival – There is simply no evidence that Marlowe survived in France or Italy. His presence there, for many years, would obviously have been remarked upon and have necessarily left a paper trail. The difficulties in his writing for the London stage, with the need of any author to know the availability and talents of the actors and the mood of the audience, seem insurmountable if Marlowe lived in a foreign country, where correspondence would take weeks to arrive. Marlowe, moreover, had no known connection with the Lord Chamberlain's/King's Men – which was founded after his stabbing – but had apparently written his plays for the Lord Admiral's Men, the rival theatre company.

6

Mary Sidney Herbert
Countess of Pembroke

Mary Sidney (1561–1621) was a well-known writer and literary patron, and the sister of Sir Philip Sidney (1554–86), the poet, diplomat, and soldier who wrote *Astrophel and Stella*, a renowned early sonnet sequence. Mary Sidney was sometimes mentioned in the earlier anti-Stratfordian literature as part of a wider circle of writers who allegedly wrote Shakespeare's works, but was never noted as a possible single author of Shakespeare until the 2006 publication of *Sweet Swan of Avon: Did a Woman Write Shakespeare?* by Robin P. Williams. With the possible exception of Queen Elizabeth, she is the first woman to be seriously proposed as the real Shakespeare. She was born near Bewdley, Worcestershire, the daughter of Sir Henry Sidney (1529–86) and Lady Mary (*c.*1539–86), the daughter of John Dudley, Duke of Northumberland. Her father was a close associate of King Edward VI and her mother had been a close friend of Queen Elizabeth. Her old aristocratic family was closely related to Lady Jane Grey, to the Earl of Leicester (the Queen's favourite), and to just about every high aristocratic family in the country. Mary Sidney was given a remarkable education at home for a woman, and was fluent in French, Italian, Latin, and possibly in Greek and Hebrew. In 1577 she was married to the newly widowed

Henry Herbert, second Earl of Pembroke (*c.*1538–1601), one of the wealthiest English landowners, by whom she had four children. The most notable of these were William Herbert, later third Earl of Pembroke (1580–1630) and Philip Herbert, Earl of Montgomery and later fourth Earth of Pembroke (1584–1650), the 'incomparable pair of brothers' to whom the First Folio was dedicated. Mary Sidney lived chiefly at Wilton House, a famous country house near Salisbury, where she (and her brother until his death) was renowned for her literary patronage. Among the writers who visited her there were Edmund Spenser (*c.*1552–99), author of *The Faerie Queene*, Samuel Daniel, and John Davies of Hereford. She was also an extraordinary writer in her own right, producing translations and paraphrases, especially of the Psalms, and a dialogue, *Astraea*. Her translation of *Tragedy of Antony* was a source for Shakespeare's *Anthony and Cleopatra*.

Mary Sidney and her family cross paths with Shakespeare at several noteworthy points. Pembroke's Men, an acting company which began around 1592 and lasted until about 1600, performed Shakespeare's *Henry VI* plays and *Titus and Andronicus*; some historians believe that Shakespeare may have been an actor with this company early in his career. In October 1603 she was hostess to James I and Queen Anne at Wilton House, where a play was performed by the King's Men, Shakespeare's company. A nineteenth-century tradition claims that this was Shakespeare's *As You Like It*, although there is no surviving contemporary evidence for this assertion. In August 1865, a remarkable entry appeared in the diary of William Johnson (1823–92), who added 'Cory' to his surname in 1872. Cory was a celebrated master at Eton, who was nearly appointed Professor of History at Cambridge (although he was a classicist, not an historian), and wrote the famous short poem *Heraclitus*. In 1872 Johnson (as he was) suddenly resigned from Eton, probably because of a sexual scandal involving his students. Later published by F.W. Cornish in 1897, his diary entry read: 'The house [Wilton] (Lady Herbert [its occupant at the time] said) is full of interest; above us in Wolsey's room; we have a letter, never printed, from Lady Pembroke to her son, telling him to bring James I from Salisbury to see *As You Like It*; "we have the man Shakespeare with us." She wanted to cajole the king in Raleigh's behalf – he came.' The royal Court was indeed at Wilton in late 1593. The problem with this crucial letter is that it has never been seen by anyone except Johnson (if indeed he actually saw it). Sir E.K. Chambers, who investigated the matter in 1898, was informed that 'no trace of the letter in question could then be found at Wilton', but that Lady Herbert believed 'that a copy was at the British Museum or possibly the [Public] Record Office', but it is certainly not in either place. The archives of Wilton House are today at the Wilton and Swindon History Centre at Chippenham, Wiltshire, but, again, the letter is not there. A further complication is that the King's Men were apparently touring the Midlands most of this time, although it is known that a Warrant for £30 was paid to the King's Men for coming from Mortlake, Surrey, to Wilton to present a play before the King on 2 December 1603 – but the King had (contrary to the diary entry) arrived there in October, while Shakespeare was either still an actor and manager with them, or perhaps in Stratford-upon-Avon. Since this letter, if it exists, is incomparably the most important item held by the Pembroke family, it is difficult to believe that it was lost or mislaid. Johnson's reference remains one of the great puzzles of Shakespeare scholarship. As noted above, Mary Sidney's sons were the joint dedicatees of the First Folio, although they had no other known connection with Shakespeare or his plays.

Points in Favour of Mary Sidney as the Real Shakespeare

1. She was qualified by education and connection to have written the plays – Mary Sidney unquestionably had the background and education to have written the plays despite her gender. Wilton House contained an extensive private library.

2. Her family was connected with the theatre – As we have seen, her husband was the patron of an acting company which might well have employed Shakespeare.

3. She was held in high esteem by many writers of her day – Among the other writers well known to her at Wilton was Ben Jonson. Michael Drayton actually referred to Mary Sidney as the 'Thames' fairest Swan', echoing Jonson's famous reference to Shakespeare as the 'Sweet Swan of Avon'.

4. Wilton House and the King's Men – As noted above, there is an actual, authenticated connection between Wilton House and the King's Men, and possibly with a play by Shakespeare. Whatever the accuracy of the Johnson diary, there was a definite connection. Similarly, it is an unquestionable fact that the First Folio was dedicated to her sons. She died in 1621, just when the First Folio was being compiled.

5. Shakespeare and women – Shakespeare was arguably unique in his three-dimensional depiction of women, his strong female characters, and his noting of women's activities such as cooking. This seems difficult to square with what we might expect from the son of an obscure glove maker in a Midlands town, or for that matter with an English aristocrat of the time.

6. 1601 – Mary Sidney's husband died in January 1601. This might well explain the great alteration in Shakespeare's writings just at that time.

7. A female writer – Being a woman provided an obvious motivation for remaining anonymous about the writing of plays and even poems such as *Venus and Adonis.*

Points Against Mary Sidney as the Real Shakespeare

1. A woman could not have written Shakespeare's works – Postulating a woman, however talented, as Shakespeare is carrying contemporary 'political correctness' too far. The sexual references in Shakespeare – to take one facet of this question – obviously reflect male sexuality, and it seems virtually impossible that a religious woman like Mary Sidney would have written the numerous bawdy references in the plays.
2. Mary Sidney had no connection with the theatre – If her husband was a patron of his own acting company until about 1600, it is difficult to see why Shakespeare wrote for the King's Men.
3. Essex and Southampton – Mary Sidney had no known connection with the Earl of Essex or the Earl of Southampton.
4. Facts about her life are inconsistent with Shakespeare's work – She never visited Italy or anywhere else in Europe, and did not die until 1621.
5. Her work is highly religious – Most of her translations and paraphrases are highly religious in content, and she is sometimes seen as a 'dour religious figure' (Margaret Patterson Hannay, 'Herbert [née Sidney], Mary, Countess of Pembroke', *Oxford Dictionary of National Biography*). Shakespeare seldom if ever wrote explicitly religious verse or dialogue, and his

universal humanism and humour seem incompatible with a writer or translator of dour religious works.

6. 'The man Shakespeare' – Even if the abovementioned letter actually existed, it would appear to show that Mary Sidney was *not* Shakespeare. Why would she claim to have 'the man Shakespeare' at Wilton if he was not the real author?

7. The general lack of direct evidence – As with so many other authorship candidates, there is simply no compelling direct evidence linking Mary Sidney with Shakespeare's works.

8. The 'Dark Lady' – Assuming that Shakespeare's sonnets are autobiographical presents many difficulties, and Shakespeare has been presumed to have been bisexual. But was Mary Sidney also bisexual, and the lesbian admirer of the 'Dark Lady' featured in the sonnets? This seems hard to believe.

7

William Stanley
Sixth Earl of Derby

William Stanley, sixth Earl of Derby (1561–1642) was a powerful
nobleman and a member of the important Stanley family, later
known as the 'kings of Lancashire'. He was born in London, and
was educated at St John's College, Oxford, and at Gray's Inn, and
from 1582 to 1585 spent three years in France. Just after this, he also
apparently visited Italy and Spain. In 1593–94 he succeeded to the
earldom when both his father and elder brother died. The new
earl initiated a lawsuit against his brother's widow, who, with her
daughters, had been left the whole of his elder brother's personal
estate. The lawsuit dragged on until 1610, when he gained most
of his brother's property. In 1595 he married Elizabeth de Vere
(1575–1627), the daughter of the seventeenth Earl of Oxford,
who of course is also a leading candidate as the 'real Shakespeare'.
The marriage was stormy. Stanley, like his father-in-law, was a
member of the jury of his peers which condemned Essex to
death in 1601. After 1603 he lived a fairly normal and successful
life, governing the Isle of Man and serving as Lord Lieutenant of
Lancashire and Cheshire. He died at eighty-one, having outlived
the other Shakespeare candidates. Again like other candidates,
he was associated with an acting company of his own, Derby's
Men, which mainly toured the provinces, and is known to have

written comedies (*c.*1599–1601) for the London theatres, and wrote for other companies, but had no known connection with the Lord Chamberlain's/King's Men. He was a friend of John Donne, Sir John Salusburie, Richard Barnfield, and other writers of the time, but not of Shakespeare or Ben Jonson.

Stanley was first suggested as the real Shakespeare by a Frenchman, Professor Abel Lefranc of the Collège de France, in a two-volume work published in 1918–19, *Sous le Masque de 'William Shakespeare'*, at almost the precise time that J. Thomas Looney argued the case for Stanley's father-in-law. Lefranc relied on an earlier writer, James Greenstreet, who had in 1891–92 noted that in 1599 a Jesuit spy in England had reported that Derby was 'busyed only in penning commodyes [comedies] for the common players'. Stanley's first name and his initials (W.S.) also made for a painless identification with Shakespeare. As well, Derby had visited Navarre in France, knowledge of which, Lefranc argued, was used in *Love's Labour's Lost*. Shakespeare's plays are full of references to places well known to Derby. The case for Stanley is at least superficially plausible, and still has its followers.

Points in Favour of William Stanley as the Real Shakespeare

1. He was well qualified to write the plays – He was well educated, had legal training, was a great nobleman, travelled in Europe, and was connected with the theatre. His date of birth, 1561, also aids the plausibility of his candidacy.

2. The Navarre connection – *Love's Labour's Lost* apparently contains detailed and accurate knowledge of this part of France, such as Derby might have had. He had visited the

Court of Navarre in the 1580s. The scene in *Love's Labour's Lost* with five of the Nine Worthies is a parody of a poem written by Derby's tutor, Richard Lloyd.

3. John Dee and *The Tempest* – Shakespeare was apparently familiar with the mystical writings and magical propensities of Dr John Dee (1527–1608), the famous alchemist and writer (who, strangely, coined the phrase 'British Empire' in a book on navigation written in 1577). Derby was also in contact with him and, it is argued, used him as the basis for Prospero in *The Tempest*. Derbyites believe that the island depicted in that play is not Bermuda, but a small island near the Isle of Man known as the Calf of Man, which would have been well known to Derby as the ruler of Man.

4. 'W.S.' – The initials 'W.S.' and the name 'Will' or the like are repeatedly used – it is claimed – by others to refer to Shakespeare. These also apply to William Stanley. Stanley, his supporters say, is referred to as 'Aetion' in Edmund Spenser's poem *Colin Clouts Come Home Again* (1594), who is often taken to refer to Shakespeare. 'Aetion' is the Greek term for 'man of the eagle', and an eagle is to be found on the crest of the Stanley family. He may also have been the 'our pleasant Willie' mentioned by his friend Edmund Spenser, in terms similar to those often used about Shakespeare.

5. As a Knight of the Garter, Derby either carried the canopy or stood by in reserve during the anointing of King James I at his coronation in 1603. Sonnet 125 famously begins 'Wer't ought to me I bore the canopy.' Only Knights of the Garter were entitled to do this.

6. He is one of the few candidates who lived long enough to add 140 lines to the 1622 Quarto of *Othello*, 190 lines to the 1622 Quarto of *Richard III*, and many other changes and revisions which were made to Shakespeare's early quartos.

7. According to Dr John Rollett (an advocate of Derby's candidacy to whom I owe many of these points), Derby's name appears in an acrostic in the First Folio of 1623, where the principal actors in Shakespeare's company are listed. The last letters of the names of the seven actors, starting with Augustine Phillips, spell out 'STE[A]NLEY'. The order in which these names are arranged appears to be contrived, while William Kemp's surname has been arbitrarily spelled 'Kempt' in order to provide a final 'T'.

Points Against William Stanley as the Real Shakespeare

1. The lack of direct association – There is nothing whatever to connect Derby with Shakespeare or with Shakespeare's acting company. All of the purported evidence suggesting that Derby is Shakespeare is purely circumstantial.

2. Essex – There is little to suggest that Derby was an associate or supporter of Essex. Derby's wife Elizabeth was rumoured to be having an affair with Essex, while Derby, as noted, was a member of the jury which condemned Essex to death. Nor did Derby have any particular association with Southampton. Derby was expected to serve in 1599 with Essex and Southampton in Ireland, but did not.

3. His date of death – Derby died in 1642, nearly thirty years after Shakespeare wrote his last play. Derby simply lived too long to have been Shakespeare.

4. 1601 – Nothing is known about Derby's life to suggest why his writing, as 'Shakespeare', changed radically and produced the great tragedies. According to Derby's entry by Leo Daugherty in the recent *Oxford Dictionary of National*

Biography, 'By 1601 his financial affairs stood on a fairly firm footing; in 1603 he was named to the privy council.' He was also appointed a Knight of the Garter in the same year. But whoever wrote *Hamlet, Macbeth,* and *King Lear* does not seem to have been a happy man.

5. Lord Strange – Derby's elder brother Ferdinando, Lord Strange, had an acting company which is often seen as evolving into the Lord Chamberlain's Men, Shakespeare's company, and is seen by some scholars as employing the young Shakespeare. But when Lord Strange died in 1594 and Derby succeeded to the title, he did *not* keep up his brother's patronage of this company, and had no known connection with the Lord Chamberlain's/King's Men, of which Shakespeare was a member and which performed most of his plays.

8

Roger Manners
Fifth Earl of Rutland

Roger Manners, fifth Earl of Rutland, was born in 1576 and died
in 1612. He was the son of John Manners, fourth Earl of Rutland
(d.1588) and Elizabeth (née Charlton, d.1595). Like Oxford and
Southampton, Rutland was a ward of Lord Burghley's after
his father died while he was still a minor, and was educated at
Burghley's house and at Queens' College and Corpus Christi
College, Cambridge. He was a close friend of Southampton's, who
was three years older than him. He then travelled abroad for several
years, visiting France, Germany, Italy, and Switzerland. In Italy, he
enrolled at Padua University, but fell dangerously ill, although he
became fluent in Italian. Manners was with the Earl of Essex on
his expeditions to the Azores and Ireland and entered Gray's Inn
upon his return. In 1599 he married the daughter of Sir Philip
Sidney, the niece of Mary Sidney, Countess of Pembroke, who was
also the stepdaughter of the Earl of Essex. Like Sir Henry Neville,
he was a supporter of Essex in his rebellion, and was imprisoned
in the Tower for six months in 1601 until he paid an astronomical
fine. As with Neville and Southampton, he was fully pardoned
and his fine remitted by James I in 1603. In June 1602 he was sent
as ambassador to Denmark (where he visited Elsinore) for the
christening of the Danish royal heir. From 1603 he was a favourite

of James I, who made him Lord Lieutenant of Lincolnshire. Manners was plagued by ill health, with chronic swollen legs, as well as by an endless lawsuit waged against Lord Roos over family estates. He was also impotent. He died aged only thirty-three at his great country house, Belvoir Castle, Leicestershire. Childless, he was succeeded by his brother Sir Francis Manners, sixth Earl of Rutland (1578–1632). Francis Manners does have one apparent direct connection with Shakespeare. At the Accession Tilt in March 1613, Rutland carried an *impresa* (a painted device) which had been designed by Shakespeare and his fellow actor Richard Burbage, each being paid 44 shillings for their work. (Some, however, questioned whether this was *William* Shakespeare.) As will be seen, the fifth Earl of Rutland has many direct connections with other Shakespeare candidates.

Rutland is in many (but not all) ways a strong candidate to be the real Shakespeare. Apparently the first pro-Rutland writer was a German, Peter Alvor, writing in Hanover in 1906. A Belgian writer, Celestin Demblon, followed, and then Lewis F. Bostelmann, whose *Rutland: A Chronologically Arranged Outline of the Life of Roger Manners, Fifth Earl of Rutland*, appeared in New York in 1911. More recently, émigré jurist and academic Pierre S. Porohovshikov championed Rutland in his *Shakespeare Unmasked*, published in 1940. Others followed, such as Claude Sykes's *Alias William Shakespeare?* (1947). Rutland also figures in many 'group theories' of the authorship which claim Shakespeare's works were written by several collaborators.

Points in Favour of Roger Manners as the Real Shakespeare

1. He was well qualified – Like most of the alternative Shakespeares, he was well qualified by his background,

education, connections, travel on the Continent, etc., to have written the plays.

2. He was a supporter of Essex – With the exception of Sir Henry Neville, he was the only well-known alternative Shakespeare to have been an active supporter of Essex before and during his 1601 rebellion. Shakespeare's acting company was certainly pro-Essex, and famously performed *Richard II* just before the uprising.

3. He visited Elsinore – He may have been the only alternative candidate to have visited Denmark, and specifically Elsinore. But he did not pay his visit, so far as is known, until two or three years after *Hamlet* appears to have been written.

4. He was closely associated with some in Shakespeare's circle – He certainly knew Ben Jonson. The death of his wife, two weeks after his own death, was the occasion for an elegy by Francis Beaumont. He was a friend of Southampton, known to Francis Bacon, a ward of Lord Burghley like Oxford – and so on, showing how small a world Elizabethan London appears to have been.

Points Against Rogers Manners as the Real Shakespeare

1. He was too young – This of course is the clincher. Rutland was born in October 1576, and was thus between twelve and fourteen when Shakespeare is generally believed to have written his earliest plays. Moreover, he was a student at Cambridge for several years after late 1587. By the time Rutland had reached his twenty-first birthday in October 1597, Shakespeare had, by the normal dating of his works, already written fourteen plays and his two long poems.

2. Chronic ill health – Rutland suffered from chronic ill health from at least the time of his visit to Italy in 1596, and died at only thirty-three. This does not entirely rule him out as the real author, but obviously seems inconsistent with Shakespeare's remarkable record of steady productivity.

3. No connection with Shakespeare or the theatre – Rutland had no known connection with either Shakespeare or the London theatre, or with Shakespeare's acting company. Whoever wrote Shakespeare's works must have had a good working knowledge of the London stage in general and the actors of the Lord Chamberlain's/King's Men in particular. Rutland wrote no literary works under his own name, although of course he may have consistently used a pseudonym. On the other hand, his brother and successor may have had an unusual but direct connection with Shakespeare through the 1613 *impresa*.

4. Impotence – Shakespeare's works are plainly redolent with sexual awareness, heterosexual and possibly bisexual. Rutland was known to be impotent, possibly through chronic illness, although he was (unhappily) married.

9

Sir Henry Neville

Sir Henry Neville was born around 1562 – the exact date is unknown – and died in July 1615. He was thus an almost exact contemporary of William Shakespeare. His father, also named Sir Henry Neville (*c*.1529–93), was an MP and courtier, a descendant of the illustrious Neville family of earlier times. Our Sir Henry's mother, Elizabeth, was the daughter of Sir John Gresham, a merchant who had been Lord Mayor of London, and a close relative of the famous merchant Sir Thomas Gresham, founder of Gresham College. Neville was educated at Merton College, Oxford, where he was a favourite student of Sir Henry Savile, the great scholar; from a young age Neville was noted for his learning. From 1578 until 1583 Neville accompanied Savile and some others on a lengthy tour of the Continent, including time spent in France, Italy, and Germany. In 1584 Neville was elected as a Member of Parliament and remained an MP until his death, with the exception of the period after 1601 when he was imprisoned in the Tower.

Neville lived the life of a country gentleman from his mansion, Billingbear, about five miles from Windsor in Berkshire. He was regarded as a rising man in Court circles. His father-in-law, Sir Henry Killigrew, was extensively employed on diplomatic missions by Queen Elizabeth. Neville's father remarried the daughter of Sir Nicholas Bacon, the half-sister of Sir Francis Bacon, and a relative of the powerful Cecils. From 1599 to 1600 Neville served as ambassador to France. On a brief return to England, he was persuaded to join in the ill-fated Essex rebellion of 1601 and, as a result, was sentenced to imprisonment in the Tower until he had paid off a fine of £5,000. He was imprisoned there with his close friend Henry Wriothesley, third Earl of Southampton, Shakespeare's supposed patron. Both men were released by King James I soon after he came to the throne. Neville, a popular hero, expected great things from the new king, but was continuously disappointed, and spent the rest of his life attempting to regain the fortune he had lost while he was ambassador and in the Tower. His hopes rose in 1609, when his son married the daughter of the Secretary to the London Virginia Company, nearly at the same time as the formal launch of the company (and virtually on the same day as the publication of *Shake-spears Sonnets*), but were again disappointed after the Bermuda shipwreck of 1610. Although he was a leader of what would now be termed the 'Opposition' in Parliament, he died in 1615 a disappointed man. In his last years (if not before) Neville was very friendly with Ben Jonson and with the playwrights Beaumont and Fletcher, whose *A King and No King* was dedicated either to Neville or to his son, another Henry Neville.

Neville was never proposed as the real Shakespeare until 2005, with the publication of *The Truth Will Out* by Brenda James – who originated the theory that Neville was Shakespeare – and this author, William D. Rubinstein. A number of further books advancing Neville's case have been published by Brenda James and Dr John Casson. These include James's *Henry Neville and the Shakespeare Code* (2008), and Casson's *Enter Pursued by a Bear: The Unknown Plays of Shakespeare-Neville* (2009) and *Much Ado About*

Noting: Henry Neville and Shakespeare's Secret Source (2010). The case for Neville seems to me to be by far the strongest of any alternative 'Shakespeare', and it seems astonishing that it was not made by any earlier writer.

Points in Favour of Sir Henry Neville as the Real Shakespeare

1. His life fits the orthodox chronology of Shakespeare's works perfectly and always explains why 'Shakespeare' wrote what he did – There is, as has been noted, a very clear evolutionary pattern to Shakespeare's works, with the Italianate comedies and triumphalist histories written between about 1588–90 and 1600, a major break around 1601, followed by the authorship of the great tragedies and the 'problem plays' thereafter. None of the other biographies of the authorship candidates can explain this pattern of development, *even the biography of William Shakespeare*, as was explained in the chapter discussing him. In contrast, Neville's life always meshes with the accepted chronology of the plays. In particular, Neville's life and career fully account for the great break in Shakespeare's works around 1601, when *Hamlet* was written, the very time that Neville was almost overnight degraded from a rising ambassador and courtier to a convicted, imprisoned traitor.

    It should be emphasised that Neville's life fits the orthodox chronology of the plays as they are universally dated by scholars. Unlike the case for the Earl of Oxford, one does not have to invent a new, highly implausible dating system for Shakespeare's plays to fit in with Neville's life. Indeed, the case for Neville is plausible *only* if the orthodox chronology is fully accepted.

2. Neville was fully qualified to write the plays – He came of an illustrious family (although from a branch which had declined from national power to relatively minor gentry); was a noted scholar at Oxford; visited Europe, including Italy; was multilingual and in contact with leading European scholars of the 'New Learning'; was a Member of Parliament for many years; moved in Court circles; and was a known friend of leading writers and playwrights. As a JP and major figure in Berkshire, he would also have acquired a practical legal knowledge, especially of real property law.

3. Neville was a close friend of Southampton – Neville had certainly met Southampton in early life. He spent two years beside him in the Tower of London (1601–03). They were not in 'close confinement' and presumably met on a daily basis. In the 1600s Neville was one of Southampton's closest political associates, and was often linked with him in contemporary accounts.

4. Neville was an Essex conspirator – The Lord Chamberlain's Men were known as the pro-Essex theatre company and performed *Richard II* just before the Essex rebellion. This performance took place five days after Neville met with the Essex conspirators and agreed to join them, presumably at Essex's urging. (Essex promised to make Neville Secretary of State, if he were successful.)

   In contrast, there is no known linkage between the Essex rebellion and *any* of the other authorship candidates, *including William Shakespeare*, who was probably in Stratford at this time.

5. Neville and *Shakes-peares Sonnets* – Postulating Neville as Shakespeare also offers a cogent explanation of the publication of *Shake-speares Sonnets* on 20 May 1609. They were published by Neville to commemorate the official granting

of the charter of the second London Virginia Company (23 May 1609), of which Neville was a director and on which Neville was pinning his financial hopes, and also to mark the marriage of his eldest son on 2 May 1609, to whom the first eighteen sonnets are addressed. 'Mr. W.H.' is Southampton, Neville's close friend (who had been stripped of his earldom in 1601–03 when he was in the Tower, and was simply 'Mr. Henry Wriothesley' when he was imprisoned with Neville). The celebrated, mysterious Dedication was actually written by Neville himself.

6. The 'dimme light of Nature' – The famous passage about Shakespeare writing 'by the dimme light of Nature', about which 'our heirs shall hear', was apparently written by Francis Beaumont to Ben Jonson in 1615. It is immediately followed by lines seldom quoted, that his lines are 'as free / as hee whose text was, god made all that is, / I mean to speake: what do you thinke of his / state, who hath now the last that hee could make / in white and Orange tawny on his back / at Windsor?' These lines are apparently a description of Neville's funeral, which occurred in July 1615 near Windsor. The 'white and Orange tawny' was apparently the livery (uniform) of English ambassadors to France, in which Neville was probably laid out. If this is the real meaning of these lines, it is evidence that there was seemingly an agreement in Neville's lifetime to attribute Neville's works to Shakespeare, and to depict Shakespeare as unlearned.

7. Ben Jonson and Gresham College – Gresham College, a kind of sub-university in London, was founded in 1597 as part of the will of Sir Thomas Gresham. Sir Henry Neville's father was Gresham's closest living male heir and the chief mourner at his funeral, and the rights of the Neville family in Gresham College were protected by two Acts of

Parliament. In October 1623 Ben Jonson described himself as 'of Gresham College of London, gent.' He was there, in other words, at just the time, or shortly after, he wrote the introductory material to the First Folio. What he was doing there is a complete mystery, but it might well have been that he was given an academic position there by Neville's family to prepare the First Folio.

8. Thomas Vicars – In 'An Unnoticed Early Reference to Shakespeare' in *Notes and Queries* (March 2006), Fred Schurink of the University of Newcastle-upon-Tyne discovered that Revd Thomas Vicars (1589–1638) had added the following to the third edition (1628) of a book in Greek on rhetoric, in a section discussing leading poets. In translation, it reads: 'To these, I think, should be added that well-known poet who takes his name from "shaking" and "spear", [and also] John Davies, and a pious and learned poet who shares my surname, John Vicars.' This is surely a rather startling indication that Vicars, writing only twelve years after the death of Shakespeare of Stratford, regarded 'Shakespeare' as a pseudonym – he pointedly did not use any circumlocution in naming John Davies or John Vicars. Even more remarkably, Vicars was *Sir Henry Neville's son-in-law*, having married his daughter Ann in 1622. If Neville was indeed the real author, it seems clear that Vicars was initiated into the 'family secret' after his marriage. This is also surely extremely clear evidence that someone, a few years after Shakespeare's death, knew that he was not the real author, and pre-dates the earliest supposed 'anti-Stratfordians' by 200 years.

9. Neville and Shakespeare were relatives – Mary Arden, Shakespeare's mother, was a distant relative of Lord Bergavenny (Neville's grandfather) and had a similar coat of arms (E.K. Chambers, *William Shakespeare: A Study of*

Facts and Problems, Vol. II (Oxford, 1930), pp.8–32). This may well be how they met, if indeed Shakespeare the actor and theatre-sharer functioned as Neville's frontman.

10. Handwriting and word clusters – Dr John Casson is the author of several books arguing the case for Neville as Shakespeare. In his most recent work, *Much Ado About Noting* (2010), he presents striking evidence that Neville's handwriting was clearly similar to the marginal annotations in *Halle's Chronicles*, which are also attributed by some to Shakespeare. Dr Casson has also compared ten randomly selected letters written by Neville with Shakespeare's plays, studying words used only once by Shakespeare. He found more than eighty examples of Neville using the same word in these ten letters, many of which were written in the same year as the relevant Shakespearean play or even earlier. For instance, he found the word 'muttering', used by Shakespeare only in *Othello*. *Othello* was premiered at the Banqueting House in Whitehall on 1 November 1604. Neville used the same word in a letter written from Parliament on the same day. There is no other recorded usage of the word in English between 1604 and 1607.

11. *The Encomium of Richard III* – The Earl of Southampton apparently wrote out his own version of a work entitled *The Encomium of Richard III* and dedicated his work to Sir Henry Neville. It is signed 'Hen. W.' Dr John Casson has dated it from watermarks to 1603, presumably just before or just after both men were released from the Tower. Neither Southampton nor Neville had any ostensible interest in King Richard III, and still less in a work praising him. From a Catholic background, Southampton might well have wished to praise the Catholic monarch, taking issue with the depiction of pure evil presented in Shakespeare's play. 'Hen. W.' was the way

Southampton would have been known in 1601–03, when he was stripped of his title by Queen Elizabeth following the Essex rebellion, and this also gives us a clue as to why *Shakespeares Sonnets* are dedicated to 'Mr. W.H.', probably Neville's affectionate nickname for Southampton when they were prisoners in the Tower.

12. Falstaff? – Sir Henry Neville was increasingly overweight, like Sir John Falstaff. In June or July 1599 Lord Southampton wrote to his wife that 'All the news I can send you [is] that Sir John Falstaffe is by his mrs. dame pintpot made father of a godly millers thumb, a boye that's all heade and litel body – but that is a secret.' On 26 September 1599 Neville wrote to Sir Robert Cecil that his note was shorter than usual 'by reason of some domesticall Misfortune in the losse of my Son lately born'. Southampton was a close friend of Neville's and it is possible that Southampton, who almost certainly knew Neville's authorship secret, would have referred to him as 'Falstaff', which might well have been his nickname among friends. There is no reason to suppose that Southampton ever set eyes on William Shakespeare, whose wife Anne certainly never produced a child in 1599.

13. The Northumberland Manuscript – Neville's name and motto appear to be written at the top of the Northumberland Manuscript, an Elizabethan manuscript discovered in 1867 at the London home of the Duke of Northumberland, which contains the names of William Shakespeare, Francis Bacon, and other playwrights, the names of several of Shakespeare's plays, and many illegible scribblings. It was apparently a wrapper placed around manuscripts or copies of Elizabethan works, although its author and purpose are a mystery. Why Neville's name should be at the top of the manuscript is not clear, unless he was the owner and presumably the author

of some of the works it once enclosed. The manuscript is obviously striking for actually linking Neville's name with Shakespeare (and with Bacon, his relative by marriage). Baconians have also long claimed the manuscript as evidence for Bacon as the author.

Points Against Sir Henry Neville as the Real Shakespeare

1. Neville wrote no literary works or plays – Sir Henry Neville wrote no literary works under his own name of any kind. His surviving writings consist of memoranda produced as ambassador to France or as an MP and landowner.

2. Neville was too busy to write plays – After 1604 Neville was a member of many parliamentary committees, and was presumably a very busy man during his time as ambassador to France. (In actual fact, however, he had a great deal of time on his hands in both roles. William Shakespeare was both a full-time actor and an author, went on frequent acting tours and maintained two households in different parts of England with significant business interests in both. Shakespeare, however, was not too busy to write the plays.)

3. Why the cover up? – No alternative authorship theory really explains why there was a cover up of the real identity of the author of the plays. In Neville's case, however, we may have an answer in the Beaumont–Jonson letter. When Neville was starting out, he presumably was afraid, as a young MP and a Neville, of writing political plays about the rise and fall of English dynasties and monarchs, while his authorship of works like *Titus Andronicus* and *Romeo and Juliet* would have mortified his eminent Oxford tutor, Sir Henry Savile.

4. No direct evidence – No direct, unequivocal evidence has been found that Neville was Shakespeare. If he was the real author, surely some evidence must exist. The same, of course, can be said of the other candidates.

5. No connection with the theatre – Neville had no connection with any theatre company. If there was a secret author, he must have had a continuing direct connection of some kind with Shakespeare's acting company.

Some Possible Conclusions

While evidence on all sides of this question has been presented, hopefully with fairness, a number of possible conclusions seem reasonable from the evidence about Shakespeare. First, although a strong case can be made for the orthodox viewpoint, that William Shakespeare (1564–1616) of Stratford wrote the plays and other works attributed to him, it is not an overwhelming case, and contains disturbingly little in the way of unambiguous direct evidence. Nor does it really refute the many reasons postulated by anti-Stratfordians about the implausibility of Shakespeare as author, especially the meagreness of his background and the lack of the erudition, worldly experience, possible Continental travels, and simple free time required to have written his works.

The Shakespearean candidates all have pluses; most have distinct minuses as well. In particular, the case for the current leading candidate, Edward de Vere, seventeenth Earl of Oxford, appears surprisingly weak, and (like the case made in the past by overenthusiastic Baconians) often extends into sheer fantasy. The case for Sir Henry Neville plainly appears to be both the strongest of those examined here, and that with the fewest weaknesses. Readers will, of course, have to consider all of this openly and objectively, and make up their own minds.

Select Bibliography

The most comprehensive examination of the facts of Shakespeare's life, with hundreds of documents, remains E.K. Chambers, *William Shakespeare: A Study of Fact and Problems* (two volumes, Oxford, 1930). S. Schoenbaum's *Shakespeare's Lives* (Oxford, 1991) is the standard account of what is known about Shakespeare's life, as well as of the development of anti-Stratfordianism. Good biographies of Shakespeare as the unquestionable author include Ian Wilson, *Shakespeare: The Evidence* (London, 1993), who argues that he was a secret Catholic, and Park Honan's *Shakespeare: A Life* (Oxford, 1999), probably the best of the innumerable recent thoroughly orthodox biographies. F.E. Halliday, *A Shakespeare Companion* (Harmondsworth, 1964), a Penguin book, remains a supremely useful dictionary of Shakespeare's life and works. A more recent larger-scale dictionary is Michael Dobson and Stanley Wells, eds, *The Oxford Companion to Shakespeare* (Oxford, 2001). Stanley Wells and Gary Taylor, *William Shakespeare: A Textual Companion* (New York, 1997), a scholarly work, is very useful for the recent orthodox chronology of the works. Alan and Veronica Palmer, *Who's Who in Shakespeare's England* (London, 2000), contains 700 concise biographies of Shakespeare's contemporaries.

The Oxford Dictionary of National Biography (2004) is, of course, now the standard biographical source.

Most notable anti-Stratfordian works supporting one or another candidate have been mentioned in the discussion on each above. The most significant previous general works on anti-Stratfordianism include R.C. Churchill, *Shakespeare and His Betters* (London, 1958); H.N. Gibson, *The Shakespeare Claimants* (New York, 1962); and John Michell, *Who Wrote Shakespeare?* (London, 1996). Warren Hope and Kim Holston, *The Shakespeare Controversy: An Analysis of the Authorship Theories* (second edition, Jefferson, N.C., 2009), discusses the main theories and contains a very detailed bibliography with works written as recently as 2008. Two recent detailed and cogent works concluding that Shakespeare did not write the works attributed to him are A.J. Poynton, *The Man Who Was Never Shakespeare* (Tunbridge Wells, 2011), and Katherine Chiljan, *Shakespeare Suppressed* (San Francisco, 2011).

Diana Price, *Shakespeare's Unorthodox Biography: New Evidence of an Authorship Problem* (Westport, Conn., 2001), significantly examines the many difficulties in the orthodox viewpoint. Bertram Fields, *Players: The Mysterious Identity of William Shakespeare* (New York, 2005), argues that Oxford and others wrote the plays in collaboration. Two recent books attacking anti-Stratfordianism and supporting the traditional view include Irvin Leigh Matus, *Shakespeare, In Fact* (1994), Scott McCrea, *The Case for Shakespeare: The End of the Authorship Question* (Westport, Conn., 2005), and James Shapiro, *Contested Will: Who Wrote Shakespeare?* (London, 2010). Shapiro's work received tremendous publicity – a sign of the recent re-emergence of anti-Stratfordianism – but is largely unsatisfactory in successfully engaging with the anti-Stratfordian arguments.

List of Illustrations

Page 95: **1.** Engraved portrait of William Shakespeare from the title page of the First Folio (1623), by Martin Droeshout. (© Stephen Porter)

Page 96: **2.** The earliest drawing of Shakespeare's monument in Stratford church, made by William Dugdale in 1653 and published in his *Antiquities of Warwickshire.* (© Folger Shakespeare Library)

Page 97: **3.** A view of the Bankside area of Southwark by Wenceslaus Hollar in 1647. (© Jonathan Reeve, JR1119b67pxvi 16001650)

Page 98: **4.** The Globe Theatre, as depicted in 1616. (© Stephen Porter)

Page 99: **5a.** The signature of William Shakespeare on his will, as dated 25 March 1616. (© Jonathan Reeve, JR1067b5fp306 16001650)

Page 99: **5b.** Another signature of Shakespeare's, on a legal document of 1612. (© Jonathan Reeve, JR1066b5fp300 16001650)

Page 100: **6.** The title page of the First Folio (1623). (© Stephen Porter)

Page 101: **7.** Edward de Vere, seventeenth Earl of Oxford (1550–1604). (© National Portrait Gallery, London)

Page 102: **8.** Sir Francis Bacon (1561–1626). (© National Portrait Gallery, London)

Page 103: **9.** William Stanley, sixth Earl of Derby (1561–1642). (© National Portrait Gallery, London)

Page 104: **10.** Sir Henry Neville (*c.*1562–1615). (Drawing courtesy of Dr John Casson and Andy Smith)

Index

Also available from Amberley Publishing

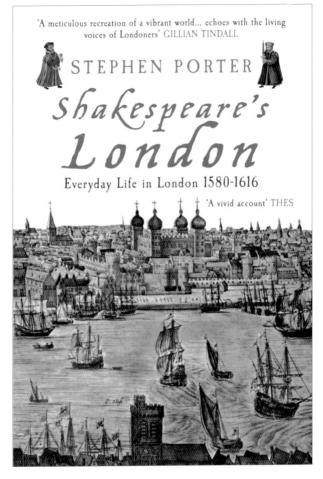

Everyday life in the teeming metropolis during William Shakespeare's time in the city (c.1580-1616), the height of Queen Elizabeth I's reign

'A vivid account' THES

'A lucid and cogent narrative of everyday life' SHAKESPEARE BIRTHPLACE TRUST

Shakespeare's London was a bustling, teeming metropolis that was growing so rapidly that the government took repeated, and ineffectual, steps to curb its expansion. From contemporary letters, journals and diaries, a vivid picture emerges of this fascinating city, with its many opportunities and also its persistent problems.

£9.99 Paperback
127 illustrations (45 colour)
304 pages
978-1-84868-200-9

Available from all good bookshops or to order direct
Please call **01453-847-800**
www.amberleybooks.com

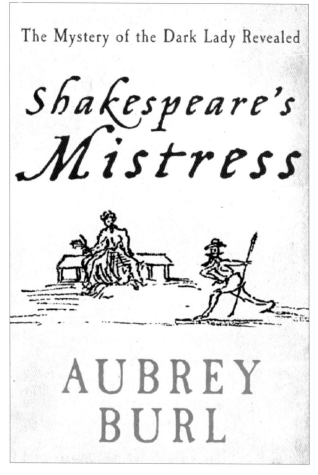